Kinetic
Contraptions

Kinetic
Contraptions

Build a Hovercraft,
Airboat, and More with
a Hobby Motor

Curt
Gabrielson

CHICAGO
REVIEW
PRESS

Library of Congress Cataloging-in-Publication Data

Gabrielson, Curt.
  Kinetic contraptions : build a hovercraft, airboat, and more with a hobby motor / Curt Gabrielson.
     p. cm.
  ISBN 978-1-55652-957-3 (pbk.)
  1. Motor vehicles—Models—Juvenile literature. 2. Airplanes—Models—Juvenile literature. 3. Ground-effect machines—Models—Juvenile literature. 4. Motorboats—Models—Juvenile literature. I. Title.

  TL237.G33 2010
  621.46078—dc22

                                                      2009025695

Cover and interior design: Sarah Olson
Photos: Curt Gabrielson

Published by Chicago Review Press, Incorporated
814 North Franklin Street
Chicago, Illinois 60610
ISBN 978-1-55652-957-3
Printed in the United States of America
5 4 3 2 1

Contents

To my parents, who took my piles of junk seriously.

Acknowledgments

Gustavo Hernandez, our magnificent co-coordinator at the Watsonville Environmental Science Workshop, was a genuine treasure in preparing, troubleshooting, honing, and giving fresh perspective on this set of projects. His enthusiasm for helping kids to learn from these sorts of projects is unbounded. The hundreds of Watsonville kids served by the Science Workshop were also invaluable in testing and giving feedback. I trust they enjoyed building the projects as much as I did. Gustavo and Fabiola Pizano also helped set up and pose for the photos (after hours!).

Thanks to Paul Doherty for checking the science content. All remaining errors are my own. Thanks to Jerome Pohlen at Chicago Review Press, for being an editor with a genuine human touch—perhaps one of the last. Thanks to Rory for the laptop on which this was written.

Like folk tunes, science projects such as these are continually being changed and improved upon as they pass hand to hand, shop to shop. I've given credit at the end of each project section if I can recall where I picked up the idea, whether or not that was its true origin.

Introduction

Blenders, hair dryers, car starters, vacuum cleaners, power drills, CD, DVD, VHS and cassette players, refrigerators, heaters and AC units, washers and dryers, air compressors, electric toothbrushes, cell-phone vibrator units, ceiling fans, and remote control cars—what do these things have in common? They are all powered by electricity, but also by magnetism, because an electric motor lies at the heart of each of them.

Electric motors are amazing devices. You put in an electric current and you get out a rotating shaft. Attach something to the shaft, and it will rotate as well. Over the 19 decades that these devices have been around, they have done a lot of work for humankind. Today, people without access to electric motors spend a lot of time and energy doing things that are effortless for you and me, such as washing clothes. In other words, no more whining when you have to move your clothes in and out of two machines that basically do all the work for you.

Large electric motors power ski lifts, pumps, elevators, some buses, and more and more family cars. You usually have to get some sort of technical degree before you get to play with these types of motors. But small is also beautiful. Nowadays you can buy motors smaller than your pinky for a few bucks. You can find the least expensive commercial motors, about the size of your thumb, for around 60 cents. You can also get one for free by ripping it out of an old toy. There is no reason not to have several of these motors sitting around your house to explore and experiment with.

I have been tinkering with small motors since I was eight years old. As I selected the projects to include, I realized that they are just the tip of the iceberg. Dozens of brilliant projects are possible with the low-cost, low-tech components and building techniques described here, so don't stop with what's in this book. Bump it up a notch, baby, and create a truly original kinetic masterpiece to call your own. But don't spend any money on it!

I'd love to hear from you if you come up with something magnificent. If it's a truly original kinetic contraption masterpiece, I'll make you famous in the next book. You can e-mail your ideas to me at information@curtgabrielson.com.

Happy tinkering!

Electromagnetic History and Accidental Science

On April 21, 1820, the Danish scientist Hans Christian Ørsted was fiddling around with some parts he used to make electricity and magnetism demonstrations. Among other things, he had wires, batteries, and a compass. Upon connecting a wire across a battery, he was startled to notice a twitch in the compass, which was laying near the wire.

This was arguably the most important discovery of the 19th century. It was the first direct connection observed between electricity and magnetism. Up until that time, the phenomena associated with these two areas, while astonishingly similar in many respects, were always thought of as separate. Today all modern motors, transformers, tube-type video screens, solenoids, electromagnets, and magnetic storage devices are made possible through our understanding of this link. Even the electric lights you are using to read this are almost surely powered by a faraway generator, a device which essentially uses magnetism in motion to create electricity.

We can learn two key lessons from Ørsted. First, **it rarely pays to have your workbench too neat and clean**—you may miss the most important discovery of your time! (Obviously, this is a message your parents must hear.) Second, **casual tinkering combined with careful observation can lead to great stuff.**

So if either your science teacher or textbook gives you the message that science happens through a lockstep process in which trained professionals traverse a well-known road toward the next great scientific discovery, you must stand and shout, "Balderdash!" A long list of earth-shaking, history-changing finds, including (among many others) X-rays and radioactive decay, small-pox vaccine, Teflon, matches, penicillin, polyethylene, glass, and DNA, were stumbled upon by fiddling and tinkering, all the while looking closely at what was happening.

TIPS FOR USING THIS BOOK AND BUILDING GOOD STUFF

◉ The chapters "Getting Started," "Basic Circuitry," "Mounting the Motor," and "Peripherals" fill you in on the low-tech elements used to build the kinetic contraptions throughout the book. You probably should at least skim those chapters first.

◉ After that, you don't necessarily need to start at the beginning. Jump right to the project that strikes your fancy.

◉ The projects are divided into easy (■☐), medium (■■☐), and hard (■■■). If you haven't built much before, start with the projects marked easy and work your way up.

◉ Look at all the photographs first, and then, if you need more information, read the words.

◉ You can learn valuable information by reading "The Science Behind It" section at the end of each project. Many other raw science and engineering concepts are in the introductory chapters and the final chapter, "Exploring Motors."

Getting Started

Tools and Materials

Many project books will begin with a clean picture of the parts you'll need to build the project all lined up neatly on the table with nothing else around. This is clearly bogus—real projects are spawned in the crucible of a good workshop packed to the gills with interesting junk of all sorts and a wealth of common supplies and materials. You simply can't do good science or engineering from a tidy set of custom selected parts laid out in a row.

In other words, you should immediately begin accumulating interesting junk to work with (if you haven't already). I'll list a bunch of things I use all the time, but any random object that you come across may turn out to be the key element for your next project. It has happened to me many times.

It pays to be *organized*, however, even if you're not neat and clean. Keep all your parts and pieces together in little boxes so that each time you to go work on something, you've got the whole range of components available to you.

Make a space for yourself to tinker and explore. It could be a little table or a corner of a room or a section of your garage. Call it your Prototype Design Lab and make a permanent PROJECT IN PROCESS sign so that your parents don't expect you to clean it up all the time.

TOOLS

Tools from the following list may be required to build the kinetic contraptions in this book. Then again, you can always improvise. As my dear old dad said, "You have to have the right tools for the job. But if you don't, you still have to do the job!"

- Drill with bits
- File
- Hacksaw
- Hammer
- Hot glue guns with plenty of glue sticks—low temperature works fine and is safer, but high temperature bonds a bit better
- Knives: box cutter, hobby knife, and razor blade
- Needle-nose pliers
- Pliers
- Ruler
- Scissors
- Screwdrivers: flat and Phillips, large and small
- Side Cutter
- Vice or C-clamps
- Wood saw

MATERIALS AND SUPPLIES

It is good to have the following stuff on hand to do these projects, and as inspiration for thousands of other projects. You can check my Web site, www.curtgabrielson.com, for more information on where to find materials.

- **Motors:** Buy one or two at an electronics shop or order a dozen on the Web. Or you can rip them out of old toys.
- **Batteries:** Cheap batteries at 99-cent stores don't last long, but they're what we use most of the time. If you screw up and leave a project connected, it will drain a high-quality, high-cost battery just as completely as a cheap one. The best option, however, is to invest in rechargeable nickel-metal hydride (NiMH) batteries and a charger. They'll last for years if you take care of them, so they

are cheaper than any other type in the long run. Even solar-powered chargers are available.

- **Electrical Wire:** Thin copper wire from phone or Internet connections is used on most of these projects. You could also use bare copper wire, but if it contacts another wire you'll have a short circuit. For the projects in the "Exploring Motors" section (page 149) you'll want magnet wire of 24 to 30 gauge. If you buy just one size, get 26 gauge. You can buy it on the Web or at a motor repair shop, or you can rip apart an old transformer or large motor. For the speed control, you can find an old toaster at a resale shop and rip the heating element wire out of it.

- **Structural Wire:** Baling wire is useful, as are clothes hangers, picture-hanging wire, wire twisty ties, pipe cleaners, and even old bicycle spokes.

- **Kitchen and Household Stuff:** Disposable utensils, cups and plates (all different types), bamboo skewers, toothpicks, clothespins, straws, paper, and aluminum foil.

- **Office Supplies:** Binder clips, pencils, paper clips (large and small), stapler, rubber bands of all sizes, tacks, push pins, and brass fasteners.

- **Corks, Film Canisters** (a dying breed thanks to digital cameras), **and Thread Spools:** In really old project books, you'll see a lot of references to thread spools. In many cases, you used to be able to substitute a film canister, but these days it is almost as easy to find a thread spool as a film canister. A few other things can fill in for these two endangered species: salsa cups, medicine bottles, and corks.

- **Wheels:** Bottle lids, film canister lids, checkers, poker chips, large beads, and wood circles cut with a hole saw.

- **Tape:** Black (electrical) is the most commonly used tape in these projects, but transparent, masking, and duct are also useful to have around.

- **Fasteners:** Nails of various sizes can be used, or for an even stronger hold you can use drywall screws and a hand drill.

- **Wood:** Three standard sizes for light construction: paint paddles (for stirring a gallon of paint—usually free at the paint shop, so grab a handful!), tongue depressors, and craft "Popsicle" sticks. For beefier projects, 1-by-2-inch furring strips are quite useful, and a small pile of scrap wood from ¼ inch to ¾ inch thick is needed for baseboards and other parts. Wood dowels ¼ inch to $\frac{5}{16}$ inch are quite useful.

- **Decorations:** Paint, markers, glitter, ribbons, colored paper, stickers, puff balls, pipe cleaners, etc.

Safety

I could list a lot of specific safety procedures, but most of the time it comes down to this: be cautious and don't be stupid. Safety should always be your first priority. If you don't put it first, you'll get a bloody finger or a damaged cornea instead of a fun project.

Most of the injuries kids have suffered at the Watsonville Science Workshop have come from hot glue and knives. Here are a few pointers for avoiding injuries:

- Wear safety glasses when using any power tool.

- Never touch the tip of the hot glue gun, and don't touch the glue when it comes out. If you do get hot glue on you, wipe it off as quickly as you can or it will continue burning. (If you do happen to get burned, you can learn a lot about the amazing function of skin as you watch it heal.)

- Always cut *away from yourself* with a knife.

- Keep your other hand away from the tool when using a knife, hammer, saw, or drill.

- Unplug something before you take it apart. Even then, capacitors may be holding a charge that could hurt you. Don't open or disassemble anything that says "Danger" or "High Voltage" on it—definitely not a TV or computer monitor.

- Get adult help if you have the least concern about the safety of a procedure. That's what they're there for.

Basic Circuitry

Two main components—batteries and motors—will make your kinetic contraptions go. To be specific, batteries provide the *energy* for your machine and the motor provides the *force*.

Electrical energy is stored in a battery. Generally speaking, the bigger a battery is, the more energy it stores. However, there is not a direct connection between the size of a battery and the *voltage* it gives. For example, AAA, AA, C, and D batteries all give about 1.5 volts. But you can bet your best wire strippers that the D battery will last a lot longer than the AAA in a given circuit. If your contraption must be lightweight, go for the smaller batteries, but understand there's a tradeoff.

Rectangular 9-volt batteries are actually six cells of 1.5 volts each—rip a dead one apart and see for yourself. (Alkaline batteries contain nastier chemicals then 9-volt batteries, so *don't* rip alkalines apart.) I've had bad luck using 9-volt batteries for motors. Such small cells just don't hold enough energy for a motor or other high-current application. Once connected, the battery meets a hasty death.

Chemicals within a battery stand ready to carry out two separate reactions: one producing excess electrons, the other consuming them. If you connect those two reactions with a conducting path, the reactions will begin and the electrons will flow from one to the other, making electricity (direct current). A copper wire works well for making the path—if you use just copper wire, an enormous gush of current will flow from one end of the battery to the other, and your battery will die within a few minutes. It may also get hot from the chemical reactions happening so fast. The wire will get hot, too, from all the collisions among those electrons cruising through it. And if the wire is too small or the wrong type, it may even melt or burn up.

If, on the other hand, you direct the electricity to flow through the motor on its way from one end of the battery to the other, the motor will turn, producing mechanical force to do work for you. Clever, eh? You can imagine how excited the first people who worked out this little trick must have been. Later in the book you'll learn more about how this trick is pulled off. For now, it's time to explore the nitty-gritty of how to make great contraptions with a motor and a battery.

Good Connections: Key to a Well-Functioning Circuit

A bad electrical connection won't let the electricity flow freely, so your motor won't be as strong as it could be. It is important for each connection to be solid. Some motors come with wires already connected to them. Others have small "ears" to which you connect wires. All simple motors have just two places to connect to, called terminals, which is convenient because a battery also has two sides. Connect one terminal to each end of the battery and your motor should spin happily. Try this basic motor circuit.

PARTS

- Electrical tape
- Knife
- Motor
- 2 connection wires
- Batteries
- 2 brass fasteners
- 2 paper clips
- Aluminum foil
- Nail

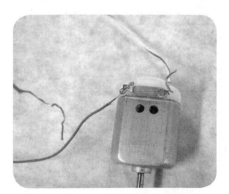

Strip a bit of insulation off both ends of each wire. The insulation is made of plastic, which the electricity can't pass through. Attach one wire to each of the motor ears, making sure the exposed copper makes a direct connection with the ear. Be careful not to twist the ears on the motor too much—if you break one off, there's only a slight chance that you'll be able to tape or solder it back on.

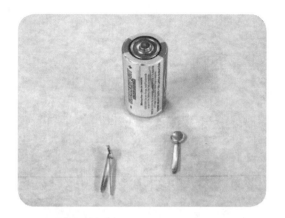

To complete the circuit, you can tape the bare wire tips to opposite ends of the battery, but often that connection won't be good. Brass fasteners make a much better connection, but small tabs of aluminum foil folded over several times will also do the trick.

The best way to attach these items onto the ends of a battery to make a strong electrical connection is to exploit the stretchiness of electrical tape. First, smash the brass fasteners flat and affix one to each end of the battery with short pieces of electrical tape.

Make sure the points of the fasteners are sticking out above the edge of the battery. Now take a longer piece of tape and wrap it as tightly as you can around the battery, end over end, stretching it hard over each pole so that the brass fasteners are squeezed tightly against the two ends of the battery.

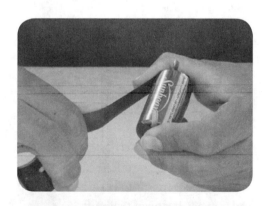

Here is the same set up, but with aluminum tabs instead of the brass fasteners.

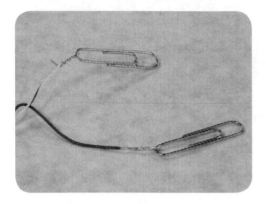

Now, twist each stripped end of the two wire leads attached to the motor around a paper clip, so that both of the "double ends" of the paper clips are free to clip onto something. That something will be the brass fasteners. Be sure the wires are twisted tightly to the paper clips—every connection counts.

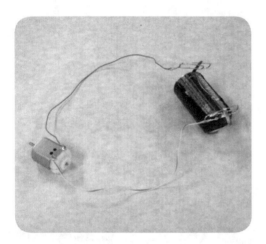

These two paper clips will be used for their intended purpose: clipping onto something thin. Don't hang them loosely over the brass fasteners or the connection won't be any good—slide them onto the upright posts. This is not only a good connection system, but also a good simple switch. When the paper clips are both connected, the motor should spin. When one is disconnected, the motor should stop.

You may also want to bend one of the brass fasteners around the paper clip at one end so that it doesn't slip off as easily.

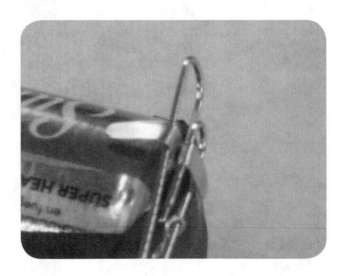

Stick something, such as a small piece of tape, onto the shaft of the motor so that you can see it turning. Then disconnect both wires from the battery and reconnect them to the opposite sides. Does your motor turn the opposite direction? (It should.) This phenomenon is called *polarity*. The battery has a positive pole that "takes" electrons, and a negative pole that "gives" electrons. The direction in which you send those electrons through the motor will determine which direction the motor turns.

If you can determine the polarity you want before you tape up the battery, it is possible to make a permanent connection on one side of the battery and leave the other side loose for a switch. Simply wad some aluminum foil over one of the wires and tape it directly to the battery. This makes one less questionable connection to go wrong.

If you can get a hold of some alligator clips, they work even better than the paper clips for connections.

More Batteries = More Energy (and Often More Voltage)

Batteries connected in a row, head to tail, add their voltage together. This is called a *series arrangement*. You can read more about that in the box below, but for now, know that you can get the motor to turn faster and stronger by adding batteries together in series.

If you want to connect two or more batteries to a motor, tape each one up separately and then connect them with wires, head to tail (that is, positive to negative).

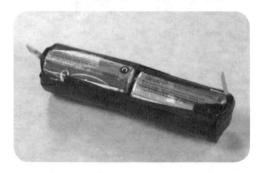

Or you can attach them together directly by aligning positive to negative ends and putting brass fasteners on opposite ends.

Notice how the black tape in the arrangement above is going the long way around the batteries. It is tempting to wrap black tape around the circumference of the batteries as shown in the photo below, *but don't do it*. If you do, the black tape often squeezes down between the two batteries, and the elasticity of the tape forces the two batteries apart so they don't touch beneath all that tape. You want a tight connection so the electricity is free to flow. Always wrap the long way.

Don't do this!

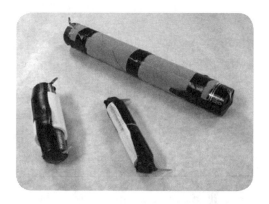

Another way to hook batteries together is to wrap something around them. Inside a tube they'll slide together nicely. D batteries fit loosely into a toilet paper tube, but you can snug it up if you scrunch it together on one side and tape it. AA batteries fit nicely inside a ½-inch PVC tube. That makes a nice holder, but it can be a bit heavy if weight is an issue for your machine. Likewise, a C battery fits into a 1-inch PVC tubing. Tubing this large gets expensive, but sometimes you can get a store to find a scrap piece for you. (After all, it's for a science project!) You can add as many batteries as you want inside tubing like this, then cut the tubing so that the end batteries stick out a bit to connect the wires.

If you want to add even more compression beyond the springiness of black tape, you can stretch wide rubber bands around the battery packs. This can be helpful even on a single battery to hold the brass fasteners tightly in place. It is sometimes tricky to get the rubber bands to stay on the rounded end of the batteries, but given a little time you can make it work. In general, if you consider these connection problems up front, you'll have less to worry about later.

Finally, if you make a project that you want to be on only while you're standing next to it, there is a fine method aligned with the all-important, ever-powerful engineering philosophy known as K.I.S.S.: Keep It Simple, Stupid. Fold one stripped end of a wire into a wad of aluminum foil and tape it to the flat end of the battery. (You can put the other side up if you want, but then the battery won't stand up as well. Change the wires at the motor side if you want to change the direction it spins.)

Put a nail or dowel into the baseboard and tape the battery to it, standing upright.

Now, when you press another wire from the other end of the circuit onto the top of this battery, it will complete the circuit. Basically, you've built a momentary switch, normally open, onto the end of your battery. You can also stack up two or more batteries and use this same arrangement. This type of battery pack is used on several projects in this book.

If you have some money to burn and time pressure or stress about putting together these simple battery packs, you can always buy a commercial battery holder. I think they're unreasonably expensive and view them as cheating. You won't find any in my workshop . . . except those I have ripped from the carcasses of other toys.

Solar Power

This book only refers to battery power, but keep in mind that you can put a solar panel on any of these projects. Of course, you'll need some sun (or a wickedly bright light) to make a contraption go when it is solar powered. Most small solar panels give low current, so the motor won't be as powerful as when used with a battery.

The best projects to power with a solar panel are the Plane-on-a-Stick (page 85), Airboat (page 67), and Wave Machine (page 130).

Parallel and Series Circuits: Batteries and Components

There are two basic types of circuits: series and parallel.

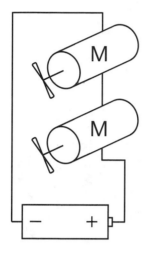

Here are two motors in series

Here are two motors in parallel

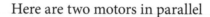

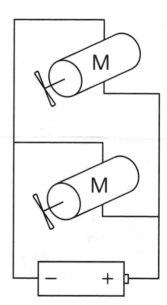

When arranged in parallel, both motors get the full voltage of the battery. When arranged in series, they share it. Because of the difference, the motors in the parallel circuit would be stronger than the series motors, but the battery would run down faster. And, if one motor burned out, the other would keep going.

The motors arranged in series would be weaker than the parallel motors, but the battery would last longer. And, if one motor burned out, the other would quit too. What happens if you stop one of the series motors from turning is bit more complicated. Try it and see!

Here are two more battery and motor arrangements.

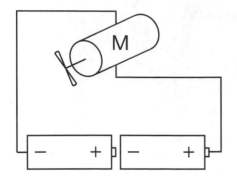

One motor with two batteries in series

One motor with two batteries in parallel

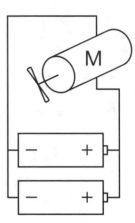

The batteries in parallel would last longer, but the motor would go slower. It gets only 1.5 volts, the same as from one battery. The batteries in series will die faster, but the motor will go faster while they last. It gets 3 volts, the sum of the batteries' voltages.

Mounting the Motor

The Roach: Motor Circuit on a Stick

Now that you know the simple circuit necessary to make the motor go, you can mount the motor wherever you want, run wires to it, and you're in business. The projects in this book will show a motor mounted on a CD, a cup, a bottle cap, and other items, but about half of them have the motor mounted on a stick. One popular high-tech tinkering system uses a device called a "Cricket." It's a small microprocessor that can coordinate the actions of speakers, lights, motors, magnets, and more. It is great fun and you can learn a lot, but buying one will set you back a couple hundred dollars.

For our projects we will build what this book calls a Roach—a motor with a battery pack and a switch. It runs when you turn it on, and is used to build a lot of great projects. And it only costs about $1.

PARTS

- Glue gun
- Electrical tape
- Hobby motor
- Connection wires
- 1 or more batteries
- 2 brass fasteners
- 2 paper clips
- ½ paint paddle

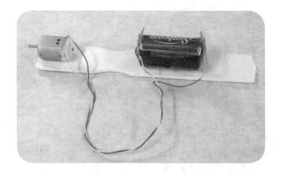

The Roach is not complicated to build. First, glue a motor onto one end of half a paint-stirring paddle, but be careful you don't get glue in the tiny holes in the motor casing. After the glue dries, check the motor by spinning the shaft with your fingers. If it doesn't spin easily, you may have glued its innards together. No biggie—often you can take the motor apart, pick out the glue, then put it back together. Once the motor is mounted, glue a battery pack (as described above) to the middle of the paddle. There's your Roach.

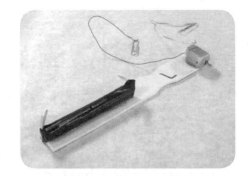

The Roach arrangement above is called an End Mount Roach. You can also mount the motor perpendicular to the stick: the Side Mount Roach.

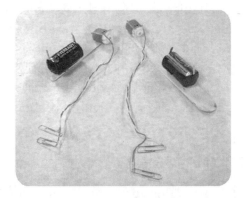

Instead of half a paint paddle, you can use a tongue depressor or even a craft stick if you're building a tiny project.

The Roach can be mounted on various different bases or chassis to create a huge variety of kinetic contraptions. You can fasten it to your device with glue, tape, rubber bands, or binder clips. Many of the projects in this book make use of the Roach. I won't tell you how to make the Roach again—the instructions will just call for an End Mount Roach or a Side Mount Roach, and suggest sizes and numbers of batteries for the battery pack. Often you'll be able to switch out the Roach from one project and use it for another one.

Soldering

If you want to be sure your electrical connections are always solid, you can solder them. This is especially useful if a project is such a success that you'll want to play with it a lot, even changing the battery when it dies.

A soldering iron or gun is a great tool, but be aware of three dangers:

⦿ A soldering iron is hot. *Way hot.* You may have accidentally touched the tip of a glue gun, or hot glue that was still hot, and thought that hurt. Well, that was nothing, my friend. A soldering iron will inflict a much more serious burn that will hurt for days and likely leave a scar for months. Needless to say, you should keep your tender digits (or anything other than solder) away from it.

⦿ Most electrical solder has lead in it. Lead can mess up your brain. Therefore, you shouldn't get it anywhere near your mouth, you should wash your hands when you're done soldering, and you shouldn't breathe too much of the smoke that comes up as you solder. Though most of the smoke you'll see is not lead, I'll bet there is some lead vapor in it, and you don't want ANY lead in your body. Zero.

⦿ If you leave the soldering iron plugged in and lying on your table with perhaps a bit of paper or cardboard below it, you can easily burn your house down.

And a final warning about the soldering iron: all three of these reasons for caution mean you should never, *never* let your little brother or sister anywhere near it.

Soldering for these projects is not difficult because you don't have to worry about screwing up some sensitive component. Just remember that the key to soldering is to get the wire and other pieces that you're hoping to stick together *hot*, then melt the solder onto them. Patience—it takes several seconds of waiting with your soldering iron touching the joint to get everything hot. If you just

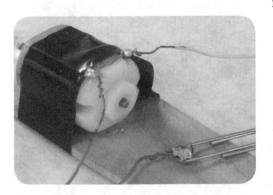

melt the solder with the iron and let it drip down onto the joint, you'll get a pathetic, ugly joint. In soldering, as in many things, beauty is a sign of quality.

Finally, while it is quite possible to solder a wire to the end of a battery, *don't do it*. On the side of a battery it clearly says not to heat it up, for it may explode or release toxic chemicals.

Connecting the Motor Shaft

Once you've got the motor happily whirring away on the Roach, you may pause to wonder how you'll ever get that tiny shaft to do anything useful. Most commercial devices use a gearbox with one gear fitted firmly onto the motor shaft. It is nearly impossible for the average tinkerer to build efficient gears, and you have to go to a specialty shop to buy a gearbox.

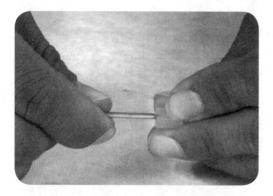

Never fear—there are low-tech ways around this problem. The easiest way is to exploit the properties of a hot glue stick to do the job. Hot glue, when cool, has a good deal of elasticity and will grab a motor shaft tightly if you jam it on. So cut a small segment of hot glue and poke a hole into the end of it with a nail.

Or better yet, drill a hole in it with a nail stuck into a drill like a drill bit.

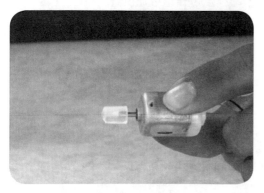

The motor shaft will then jam snuggly up into the glue stick.

Be careful to drill the hole as straight as possible so that the glue stick segment doesn't wobble when it spins. Your glue stick segment should spin together with the motor shaft as one. Most of the projects here use this low-tech element.

Propellers and Impellers

One thing you can do with a glue stick segment connected to your motor shaft is to attach a bent piece of plastic to it in order to move air or water. This creates a propeller, used in several projects here. The Fan project (page 99) pushes air to your face. The devices in the Air and Water Machine chapters push off a fluid to get force to go forward.

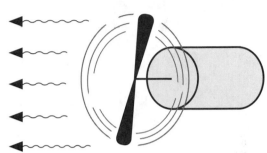

If the piece of plastic you use for a propeller is flat, it will slice through the air quickly but the air will not move. A propeller must be bent in such a way that the tips "scoop up" fluid (either a gas or a liquid) and throw it perpendicular to the plane of rotation of the propeller.

PARTS

- Knife
- Small nail, with drill if available
- Plastic soda bottle, 2-liter is better
- Glue stick segment
- Thumbtack

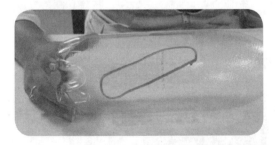

A few years ago, I stumbled upon a slick way to build a propeller: if you cut a propeller out of a plastic soda bottle at a slight angle, the curving bend will be already present in the piece that comes out.

The photo above shows a 2-liter bottle with a large propeller for a fan or Airboat drawn on it. If your machine is pushing on air, you need a bigger propeller. You don't want it too long (and heavy) though, or the motor will not have enough power to turn it fast. These motors are made for high speeds and are weak at low speeds. Propellers in water don't have to be as large—water is denser, so you don't have to push as much of it to get the force you need.

Once you've got the propeller piece cut out, fasten it to the end of the hot glue segment. First glue it on, and then tack it from the outside with a thumbtack. The tack alone may let the propeller spin loosely; the glue alone may fall off. Together they are unstoppable.

Many of the projects in this book use the propeller assembly.

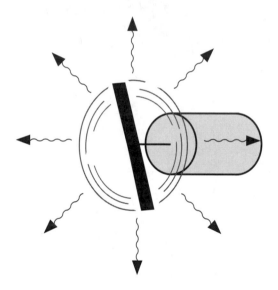

Unlike a propeller, an impeller throws fluid out from the center.

To make an impeller, cut a glue stick segment and drill a hole for the shaft in one end, as described previously. On the other end, use a knife to make a slit about ¼ inch deep. This is a bit risky, but if you hold the glue stick over the edge of the table as is shown in this photo, you won't cut your fingers if the blade slips.

Cut a flat rectangle of plastic from a scrap cup or bottle. Slide this into the slit on the glue stick segment. If it seems loose, you can glue it in place. The impeller is now finished.

The Pump (page 140), Tornado (page 103), and Snow Globe (page 107) projects use an impeller, each with a slightly different arrangement.

Drive Systems

Propellers and impellers are called *direct drive systems*, because they are attached directly to the shaft of the motor. Most light aircraft and pumps use direct drives. You can also stick a wheel directly onto the shaft of the motor, and you'll have a direct drive wheel. But a direct drive is often not good enough. A hobby motor spins fast, but sometimes you want it to spin slowly. And sometimes you'll want more force (or torque) from the motor than what the shaft gives directly. You'll need a more complex drive system, which you can make using a rubber band as a belt.

Loop a rubber band around the shaft of the motor and then around some other cylinder—a film canister, bottle, or cork—that is parallel to the motor shaft. With this assembly, you can make things turn slower and with more torque than you

can with a direct drive. You'll still want to stick the short segment of hot glue, pre-drilled with a nail hole, on the tip of the shaft in this arrangement to prevent the rubber band from slipping off.

It may not seem right, but you usually want to use thin, spindly rubber bands. Thick ones generate too much friction between the motor shaft and cylinders. Thin ones also have a larger range of stretchiness at the right tension, and you'll want fairly low tension. If you put too much tension on the shaft, the motor just stops. These hobby motors you're dealing with are not mega-power engines. It is best to use a rubber band that has a square cross section (as opposed to flat) so that it can twist and roll over itself without too much difficulty. Round would be better, but those are not easy to find.

Rubber-band drives are used on the Transmission Car (page 57), Spinning Pinecone (page 116), and Paddlewheeler (page 73), among others. You have to put the system together carefully and make sure the motor's shaft is more or less parallel to the cylinder that it's turning. This will prevent the rubber band from riding up on the section of glue stick at one end of the shaft, or the motor casing at the other end. It is easy to do this by changing the angle and position of the Roach.

Transmission Physics

Transmissions transmit (that is, take) the force of a motor shaft to another shaft. They can also change the speed and force of the rotation. They are used in cars as well as many bikes and other machines. Motors are generally built to run at a small range of speeds and don't work well at other speeds. A transmission takes a given input speed from the "driver" shaft and puts out a range of speeds to the "driven" shaft.

The rubber-band drive is a transmission. The shaft of the motor is the driver and the bottle or can is the driven shaft. If you drive a large bottle with a rubber band around the tiny motor's shaft, that bottle will have a much lower angular speed than the motor does—that is, it will turn fewer times each second than the motor's shaft does. The linear speed along the edge of the bottle is, on the other hand, the same as the linear speed along the edge of the motor shaft. That's because the rubber band (except for minor slippage) moves around the outer edges of both of these spinning cylinders.

You can understand the basic physics of rotational motion by thinking of a carousel. If you ride the horse near the outside of the carousel, you'll travel a longer distance than if you ride a horse closer to the center. Since both horses go around together, the outside horse must be going faster. (I could make the same comparison to the inner and outer edges of a record player, but you've probably never seen a record player, and a black box usually conceals a CD reading mechanism. Beware of black boxes—as the folks at *Make* magazine say, if you can't open it, you don't own it!)

The linear speed at the waist of the bottle is important, because if the bottle is the wheel of a vehicle sitting on the ground, that will be the linear speed of the vehicle across the ground. To change the speed of a vehicle without changing the speed of the motor, you have to use two wheels or pulleys on the same shaft. You can do that on the Transmission Car (page 57) by changing the position of the Roach and putting the rubber band around the neck of the bottle. The neck is one pulley and the waist of the bottle is the other. The car will go much faster if you do this.

However, you don't get something for nothing. The faster the transmission makes the car go, the less force it can give. A Transmission Car with the motor driving the neck of the bottle will not be able to accelerate as fast, or climb as steep a hill, as a car with the motor driving the waist of the bottle.

This same arrangement is commonly used in bigger machines with gear and belt systems, including those on a car or bicycle. On a geared bike, the pedal is the driver and the back wheel is the driven. Here are the rules according to the laws of mechanics:

With a given size driver gear:

⊚ The smaller the driven gear, the faster the driven shaft will spin.

⊚ The larger the driven gear, the more force will be given to the driven shaft.

With a given size driven gear, the opposite is true:

⊚ The smaller the drive gear, the more force will be given to the driven shaft.

⊚ The larger the drive gear, the faster the driven shaft will spin.

But don't take my word for it—check it out for yourself next time you ride a 10-speed.

Peripherals

Clothespin Switches

As mentioned before, the paper clip clipped to the brass fastener on the standard battery pack makes a fine switch. But sometimes you may want a better switch. You can buy these switches commercially for a few bucks each if you want to squander your money on such fleeting pleasures, but I'm against it. Instead, clothespins can be used to make the three types of reliable switches:

1. **Standard Switch:** Sometimes called a Single Pole, Single Throw, or SPST, it is either on or off, and stays where you put it.

2. **Momentary Switch, Normally Closed:** This switch is spring-loaded to the "on" position, with the current running in the circuit. When you push on this switch, you open the circuit and the motor stops turning.

3. **Momentary Switch, Normally Open:** This switch is spring-loaded to the "off" position, with no current flowing through the circuit. When you push on this switch, you complete the circuit and the motor starts turning.

PARTS

- 2 clothespins
- Hot glue gun
- Aluminum foil
- Connection wires
- Paper clip

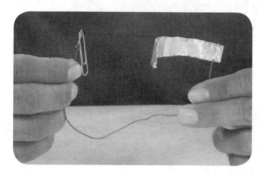

You'll first learn to build the third switch, which is used on the Bubble Maker (page 136). Take the two wires that will go to the switch and strip the insulation from both ends, a bit longer than usual, maybe 2 inches. Fold one bare wire into a piece of aluminum foil. The unfolded foil should start out around 3 inches square, then end up about 2 inches long by ½ inch wide. Fold the foil in such a way that the wire bends over itself inside and doesn't easily slide out.

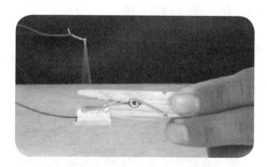

Wrap that tab of foil carefully around one handle of a clothespin.

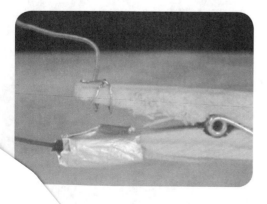

Wrap the other end of the wire around the other handle of the clothespin directly above the foil.

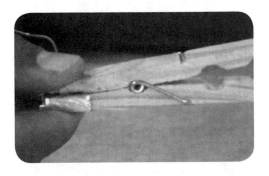

You may want to hot glue one or both of these wires in place on the clothespin handles, but be careful not to get any glue between the two surfaces where they have to make contact.

When the clothespin handles are squeezed together, the single wire contacts the foil tab and the circuit is completed. It is momentary, so when you let go the circuit goes off. This is convenient because you'll never leave it on by accident and drain your battery.

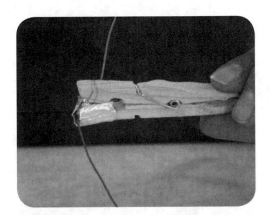

Now here's how to build the second switch, which has few applications in this particular book. Wire it just like switch three, but at the other end of the clothespin (its jaws). This switch's connection is normally closed, meaning the motor will spin, sapping energy from the battery, until you squeeze the clothespin handles and break the connection to stop it. You can see why it is not as useful.

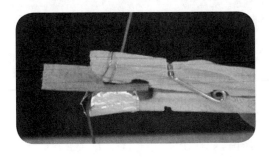

Finally, there's switch number one, which will explain why I bothered to show you the second one. If you put a small tab of paper or cardboard or craft stick between the jaws of the clothespin in switch two, the circuit will be open, and the motor will be off. Take the tab out and the motor spins. (You can think of a clever place to put the tab when the project is running so that you can find it again when you want to stick it in to turn everything off.) This is like a normal light switch that stays off or on when you flick it. A nice feature of this switch is that the spring of the clothespin is pressing hard on the connection, so you know it will be good and tight.

Keep in mind that while these switches can be handy and make your project easier to use, when you put a switch into a circuit you're introducing at least three more connections that can potentially cause problems. Sometimes the old paper clip is good enough.

Hot Glue and Electrical Connections: Dysfunctional Partners

Many a project with great potential has failed miserably when hot glue was used to make an electrical connection. Hot glue is plastic and therefore an insulator. If you glue a wire onto the end of a battery, for example, the glue will likely coat the wire and completely insulate it from the battery so that no current will flow. If you get even a tiny blob or string of hot glue across the area you wish to connect, it will introduce the demons of irregular, unpredictable, bad connection to your circuit.

Two-Tack Paper Clip Switches

PARTS

- 2 thumbtacks
- Board
- Hammer
- Paper clip
- Connection wire
- Brass fasteners
- Cardboard

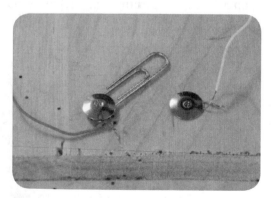

This sort of switch is a classic in low-voltage tinkering applications. Two tacks are stuck into a piece of wood, close together, each with a wire wrapped around under the head. One gets a paper clip also under the head.

The tacks are then hammered down snugly, ensuring a good connection between tack and paper clip, but still allowing the paper clip to turn. When the clip makes contact with the other tack, the circuit is on. When it doesn't, the circuit is off.

If your paper clip or tacks are painted, you may have to sand the paint off to reach the conductive metal. This switch is nice if you already have a chunk of wood in your project. Alternatively, this can be done with brass fasteners through a piece of cardboard.

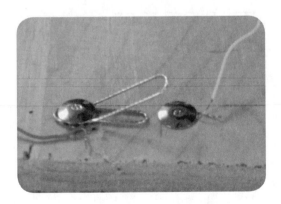

Finally, this design can be modified to be a Momentary Switch, Normally Open if you bend the paper clip up a bit so that it only touches the second tack when you press it down.

DPDT Switches

I'll describe one more type of switch here, the most complex of all, and a bit of a trick to build. The purpose of this switch is to reverse the direction of the motor. You already know that you can do this by changing the circuit's polarity, that is,

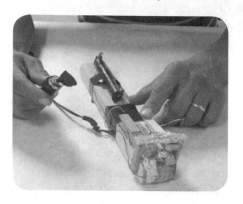

by switching the wires on opposite sides of the battery. This is exactly what happens inside a Double Pole Double Throw (DPDT) Switch. You'll want a DPDT Switch if you need to easily reverse a car or boat or spinning machine you've made. It's nice to have, and people are impressed when you flick a switch and the whole thing reverses.

"Double Pole" means you're controlling two different places in the circuit—in this case, the two poles of the battery. "Double Throw" means that you can connect those two poles in two different places. Here is the schematic for a DPDT switch connecting a motor and battery:

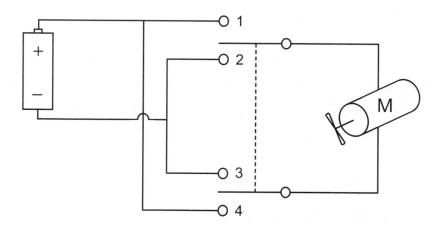

The two bars connected by the dashed line either move up and make contact with points one and three, or move down to make contact with points two and four. When they're in the center, everything is off. When they are up, connected to one and three, the positive (+) pole of the battery is connected to the top of the motor and the negative (–) to the bottom. When they are down, the opposite connection is made. Trace the circuit with your finger to convince yourself that this is true. Then you can test yourself by trying to draw one without looking at the schematic. (By the way, self tests are much more useful than any test that a teacher may give you.)

Here is how to make a slick version of a DPDT Switch using two clothespins wired in the second arrangement with an additional bar above the jaws. It is shown here connected to a test motor with a piece of tape on the shaft to show which way it is turning.

PARTS

- Hot glue gun
- 10-inch long piece of 1 x 2 wood
- 3 clothespins
- Craft stick
- Aluminum foil
- Connection wires
- Battery pack
- Motor

To make this switch, start with a 1-by-2-inch stick of wood and make a frame at one end, as shown here. The upper bar is a length of craft stick, and the two uprights on either side are halves of one side of a clothespin. Hot glue them all on. The frame should stand about ¾ inches tall, or just higher than the clothespin jaws.

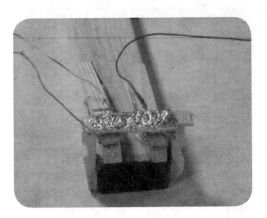

Wrap the top bar with aluminum foil already connected to a wire, and glue the two clothespins into position, outfitting them with stripped wires around their upper jaws. Make sure these wires are tight and not going to slip off. You can hot glue them into place but only on the side of the jaw, since they have to make contact above and below.

The lower foil piece is then bent as shown, and then glued carefully across the bottom jaws of the clothespins.

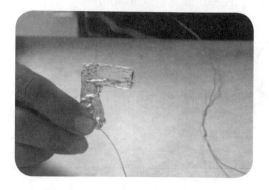
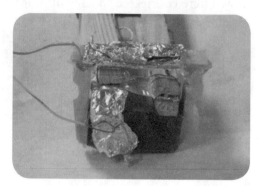

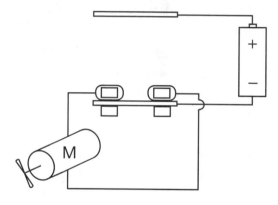

The wire from the lower foil bar will connect to one side of the battery pack, and the wire from the upper bar will connect to the other side. This will leave the two wires coming from the clothespins' jaws to connect to the two wires of a motor. In the off position, both clothespin jaws are down and the circuit is open.

When one of the clothespins opens, it disconnects from the foil bar below the jaw and connects to the foil bar above the jaw. This completes a circuit through the motor. The schematic shows the bottom of the motor now connected to the positive side of the battery.

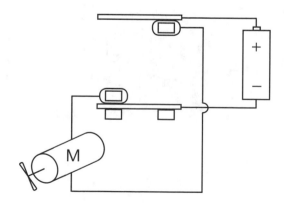

Let go of that clothespin and open the other to complete the circuit the other way, sending the current through the motor in the other direction. The schematic shows the top of the motor now connected to the positive side of the battery.

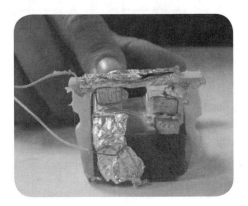 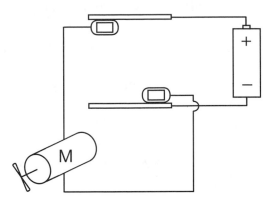

This model has the advantage of being momentary. You'll never accidentally waste your battery this way.

Most DPDT Switches can be wired with the battery's poles connected to either set of two wires. In this switch, it is critical to have the battery connected to the top and bottom bars, and not to the two clothespin jaws. Check it out. In default position, the two upper jaws are connected together because they're pressed against the bottom bar. For the motor, it doesn't matter that the two leads are connected together. If, on the other hand, you connect the battery's leads to the two clothespin

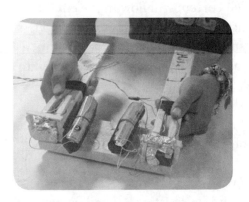

jaws, the default position would have your battery short circuited and soon dead. (I did this the first time I put it together, but I noticed the batteries getting hot before they had completely spent themselves.)

The photo here shows a Double DPDT Switch, which can be used to control two motors, such as in the advanced Transmission Car and others. Of the four wires coming off each of the DPDT Switches, two go straight to the battery packs. Two separate packs are used so that each motor is independent of the other—that is, one can't suck up all the juice. You can mount the battery packs between the switches so the kinetic contraption doesn't have to carry them. The other two wires from each DPDT Switch head down to power the motor on the mechanism below. You can see they are taped onto the switch handle. This is called *strain relief*—you can tug on the wires, but it doesn't mess up the connections.

Once again, you can buy a DPDT switch for a few bucks or extract one from a dead device, and this time it may be worth it. Making one is fairly complex, and it's difficult to make them dependable. You'll recognize this switch if you run across it because it has six terminals (places to hook wires to it). Wire it like this.

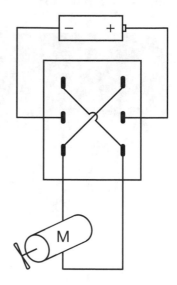

Many commercial DPDT switches have an off position between the two other connections. This is nice, and if yours doesn't have this you'll need another switch of some sort, or you can just disconnect the battery.

I was inspired for this switch by an ultra-cheap wired remote control car I bought—two for $1!—that had a similar arrangement.

Toaster Wire Rheostat

You may have seen a dimmer knob on a light, or a speed dial on a fan. The electrical component underneath is called a *rheostat*, *potentiometer*, or *variable resistor*. Resistance, measured in units called *ohms*, is a property of each part of a circuit. Resistance helps determine how much current will flow in the circuit when a given voltage is applied. More resistance will result in less current and less resistance allows more current. When using small motors you'll normally want as much current as you can get, so there is no reason to put any more resistance into the circuit.

In some cases, however, you may want to slow your motor down. You can put down several dollars of your hard-earned money and purchase a low-ohm rheostat (25 ohms usually works, though 10 ohms would be better) that will do the job. Or you can do the same job by finding a piece of resistance wire. This kind of wire is different from the copper wire you will use for the rest of the circuits here. Copper wire has a very small amount of resistance, small enough that you can assume it has no resistance at all in the circuits described here. Resistance wire of the type we use has about one ohm per inch. Six inches of it is enough to control a small motor in most applications.

It just so happens that this sort of wire is used in toasters. If you peer into a common toaster when it's on, you'll see the red hot coils of wire that are creating heat. Those are the ones you want. Unplug the toaster and rip them out. Wait, wait, NO! Not the toaster in your kitchen—find a used or broken toaster at a yard sale or a second-hand store and rip the resistance wire out of that one. Toasters are quite safe when they're cool and unplugged.

Connect the resistance wire onto the end of another wire in the circuit. Then, to control the motor speed, simply press the resistance wire in different places onto the battery. When connected all the way at the end (the longest distance), the motor goes its slowest. When connected in the middle of the resistance wire, the motor will go faster.

If you connect to the battery at the junction of the resistance wire and copper wire, no electricity will have to travel through the resistance wire, so the motor will be going full speed.

You can connect one wire to the resistance wire with a paper clip or alligator clip. This way you don't have to hold it.

Land Machines

Ever since the invention of the wheel, we humans have been working to get some other power source to turn it for us. As I write this, the two-seater Tesla Roadster all-electric sports car is doing 0 to 60 in less than four seconds, and can go 220 miles on one charge. Charge it up with an array of solar panels and you'll have free transport for years. The Roadster will set you back about $100,000 though. You can have fun for quite a bit less than that.

The following land-cruising kinetic contraptions come in all sizes: one-, two-, three-, and more wheelers. The Three- and One-Wheelers have direct drives, which limits their strength. The Two-Wheeler and the Transmission Car have rubber-band transmissions that allow you to trade the speed of your motor for a bit more force. If you put two motors on, you can even craft a remote-control device.

Three-Wheeler

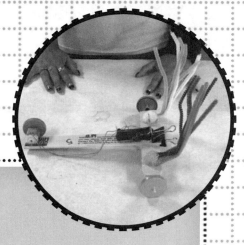

PARTS

- Glue gun
- Tape
- Side Mount Roach, 1 or 2 AA batteries
- ½ paint paddle
- Drinking straw, the fatter the better
- Bamboo skewer
- 3 wheels (film canister lids, checkers, poker chips, etc.)
- Medium binder clip

Start with a Side Mount Roach (page 22). Poke a hole in one wheel and stick it on the motor shaft. Glue it on the outer side if it is at all loose.

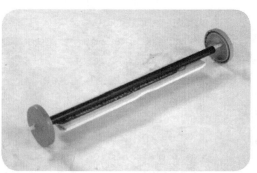

Make the back wheels by gluing or taping a straw to a half a paint paddle. Make sure the straw sticks out beyond the paddle so it will prevent the wheels from rubbing on the sticks. This will make the car roll smoothly with less friction. Slide a bamboo skewer through the straw and poke it through the other two wheels. If you have to glue the wheels to make them stay, glue *only the outside* so the glue doesn't foul up the straw bearing.

Clip the back wheels to the Roach. Connect it up and be prepared to chase it.

You can get some steerage by pivoting the Roach. There are problems with this, however, explained in the science section.

Try changing the size of the drive wheel. If you put a smaller wheel on the front, it should have a bit more torque, that is force, but a larger wheel will make it go faster when it does get going.

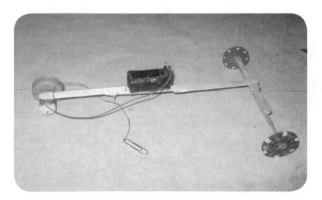

You can modify this design however you like. You can make the body from cardboard or thin wood, too. Just leave a place in front for the wheel to touch, and keep the whole thing light. Here is a photo of a Stretch Limo someone made.

The Science Behind It

You may notice that while this car's got speed, it lacks power. In fact, to quote my grandpa referring to an old tractor he had, it couldn't pull itself off the toilet. This car has no transmission. Its direct drive arrangement makes it one of the simplest vehicles you can build, but most hobby motors are not made to provide high force, or torque, at low speeds. Once it gets going, it gets more power and can go quite fast. It is like a car with only one gear, and that gear is fourth. (See the Transmission Physics box on page 28 for more information.)

If you have a stick shift car, and your parents are game, have them try to start the car moving in fourth gear. It may not even work; the engine may die. At the very least, the engine won't be pleased with this little experiment. Normally you start in first, then progress to second, third, fourth, and then maybe fifth or overdrive. Automatic transmissions do all that for you. You can set the automatic transmission to two or one to restrict it from going higher, but it always starts in first. If you have a ten- (or more) speed bike, you can put the chain on the largest gear in front and the smallest gear in back and try to peel out. You'll probably find it impossible. Some bike messengers I know leave their bikes in the highest gear if they haven't locked them up. Potential thieves will hop on, give it all they've got, but get nowhere.

If your Three-Wheeler doesn't turn sharply, it is likely because the back wheels are fixed to each other and therefore always turn at the same rate. If a car is turning a corner, the wheel on the outside of the turn has to go farther, and thus faster, than the one on the inside. Real cars (and ATVs, trucks, tractors, etc.) have a *differential* that allows the wheels to turn at different speeds. You could design one for this car too if you put your mind to it.

Over the years, I've seen innumerable students at the Watsonville Science Workshop pursue the direct drive car. Together we came to this design that works well despite the low torque.

One-Wheeler

PARTS

- Glue gun
- Drill
- Tape
- Plastic bottle with lid, 1.5 to 2 liter (larger ones work better)
- Motor, with wires and paper clips
- Battery pack, 1 AA or C battery
- Weight, about the same as a motor and battery

Start this project by gluing the battery pack directly to the side of the motor, perpendicular to the motor shaft. Wire up the motor with two paper clips at the ends of the connection wires.

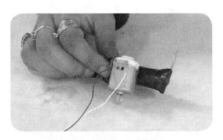

Drill a nail hole into the center of the lid.

Jam the motor shaft in from the outside, and squirt a mound of hot glue onto it from the inside.

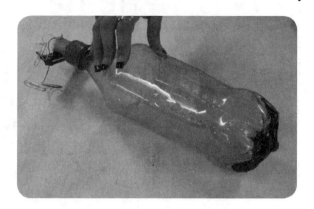

That will take a while to cool, but when it does, twist it back onto the bottle. Glue or tape weights onto the bottom of the bottle so that it doesn't tip over with the weight of the motor and battery.

Hook up the One-Wheeler and let go. It should start rolling, maybe with a little push. It needs an utterly flat surface—this is no power monster. It does tend to go straight, with the right bottle. Find a long hall or gymnasium and it will go its full length. You can put the cap on other bottles of different sizes and shapes and transfer the weights to see what happens. You can also put it in the water—experiment!

The Science Behind It

This project and the one that follows run on strange principles not often seen in everyday life. The closest you'll come to this method of transport is balancing on a large spool or ball, and then walking forward and having the spool or ball go backward. (The first several dozen times you generally end up on your butt on the ground.) Another example is a hamster ball or a hamster treadmill. The point is, when you have only one wheel, you can still use the pull of gravity to get force, or torque, to start motion.

When the motor begins to turn, the motor and battery receive torque in one direction, and the bottle in the other. The motor turns ever so slightly and the battery swings up a bit. Gravity pulls down on the battery, and it tends to swing back to the bottom. The bottle, on the other hand, is symmetric, so as it rolls, gravity doesn't tend to pull any part of it always to the bottom. So it will roll forward, and the battery will return to the bottom. As long as the battery has energy, the torque continues, and so does the motion.

Two-Wheeler

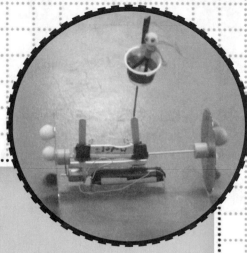

PARTS

- End Mount Roach, two AA batteries
- Glue gun
- Knife or scissors
- Rubber band, very small
- ½ paint paddle
- 2 craft sticks
- 2 CDs
- Cork
- 2 small binder clips
- Drinking straw
- 2 bamboo skewers
- Salsa cup

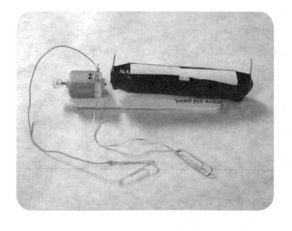

Start with the End Mount Roach (page 22). Shown here are two AA batteries in a ½-inch PVC tube section. If you make the Roach short, the car can be short. Make sure the motor shaft is sticking out far beyond the end of the paint paddle. Then attach a glue stick segment onto the tip of the motor shaft to keep the rubber band from slipping off.

Cut another section of paint paddle the same length as the Roach. Cut a section of drinking straw about half an inch longer and tape it on. It should stick out over both ends. Take care not to smash the straw too tightly under the tape.

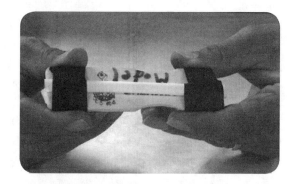

On the other side, use hot glue to attach two small binder clips as shown. You should be able to still squeeze the handles to open them.

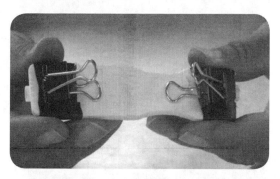

Slide two craft sticks into the binder clips. Glue the other ends to the Roach. This is the Two-Wheeler's chassis, or body.

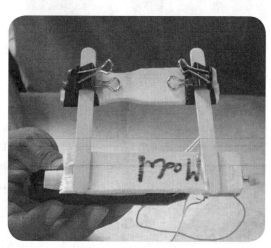

Make the wheels by cutting a cork in half and carefully gluing one half exactly to the center of both CDs.

Poke holes into the center of each cork segment. Jam one end of the skewer into each one. Before you put the second wheel on, slide the chassis and the rubber band onto the skewer. Push the chassis all the way to the wheel on the motor side and loop the rubber band down over the motor shaft. The straw, not the paint paddle section, should rub against the cork for minimum friction resistance.

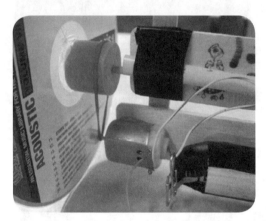

Slide the craft sticks up or down until the rubber band is tight but the chassis is not dragging the ground. Hold the car up by the chassis, connect the motor, and see if the wheels turn. Here you will know if you got the right sized rubber band. If it is too loose, the motor shaft will spin without turning the cork. Too tight, and the motor shaft will not turn.

You may have to go find another rubber band, bigger or smaller, but here are two modifications to try. First, if it is too tight, stretch it as far as you dare without breaking it. Often it will loosen up quite a bit. Or, if the rubber band is too large, you can actually cut it and carefully retie it to make it smaller. Sometimes the knot will get in the way and stop everything from moving, but sometimes it will work.

It is also important to get the motor shaft parallel with the skewer. Do this by adjusting just the binder clips one at a time, tilting the Roach until you get the right angle. When the two are parallel, the rubber band will not ride up on the glue stick segment or on the motor casing and will not fall off the cork.

If your rubber band keeps slipping off the cork, and if you already tried adjusting the angle of the Roach, you can shorten the length of the skewer until the chassis has only a fraction of an inch to slide back and forth between the corks.

Decorate it with a ridiculous crow's nest or something else.

If you make one wheel larger than the other, you'll have a car that goes around in circles. It is a bit tricky to make the chassis stay in the right place, but this can be done by adjusting the length of the straw.

Remote Control Option

PARTS

- Glue gun
- Knife
- Two-Wheeler with modified differential wheels
- CD case

- 2 clothespins
- 3 long connection wires, at least 4 feet
- Battery pack, 2 C batteries

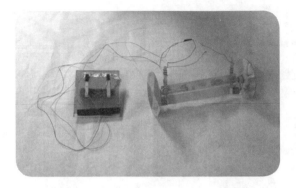

If you put two motors on this little beauty and let each wheel turn freely, you can make a hot little controllable car. What follows is one way to make each wheel turn independently of the other. This is called a differential. The bamboo skewer is chopped in the middle, and the segments are set out from the paint paddle a bit. A segment of glue stick is stuck on the ends toward the center to keep them from falling out. Two short sections of straws create the bearing. (It is also possible to glue a bamboo skewer to the paint paddle chassis and drill large holes in the corks at each CD to allow them to turn around the skewer.)

Long wires extend up from each motor. These will hook to the switch.

You could run four wires—two from each motor—to the double DPDT Switch (pages 36–40) and have full control of each motor, forward and reverse. The following switches are a lot easier to build and give you control of each motor either going forward or stopping. (This car turns so sharply that you can get by without a reverse.)

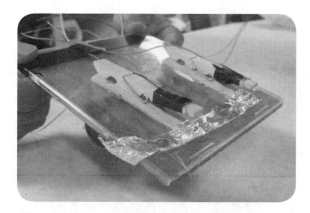

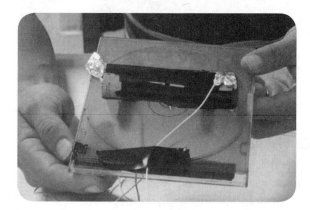

The switches are mounted on the top of a CD case and the battery pack on the bottom. The switches are two clothespins wired with the Momentary Switch, Normally Open arrangement (pages 31–32).

The stripped wire twisted around the top handle of each clothespin goes to one lead on each motor. The foil strip across the bottom handles of the clothespins connects to one pole of the battery pack. The other pole of the battery pack is connected to both other leads of the motors. Thus there are only three wires leading from the switches to the motors.

Here is the schematic. Follow the current with your finger as you close each switch.

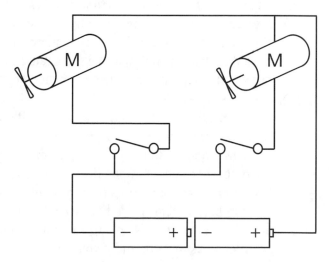

The remote control Two-Wheeler is a blast to use. The longer the wires, the farther you can go without moving. Of course, it doesn't touch the experience of a normal remote control car, but, hey, you built it, and for nothing but a bit of pocket change and a pile of scrap materials.

The Science Behind It

The sizes of the cork and the wheels determine the speed in this kinetic contraption, as you'll see more clearly in the next project. If you swap the corks for a larger circle, such as a medicine bottle, your car will be stronger but slower. Sometimes you can get the car to move when the rubber band is looped directly over the bamboo skewer. Since the skewer is about the same size as the motor shaft, this arrangement will have the wheels spinning at the same rate as the motor shaft—quite fast. But you'll pay for this speed with a near complete loss of torque; your car will be weak as a lily.

Large cars and bikes have been built with this design. They are not practical for various reasons. Turning can only be done by braking with one wheel and continuing with the other. Stopping is problematic. Try to imagine what would happen if you slammed on the brakes on this beast. It's complicated, but basically there would be a lot of swinging and rocking back and forth, perhaps even looping around the axle. You can actually see this if you hook up a remote control. If you get your Two-Wheeler stuck in a rut, and if you can provide enough torque, the chassis will spin around and around the axle without the wheels moving at all. Despite all these problems, if you do build yourself a large version of this car, you'll be the talk of the town!

Transmission Car

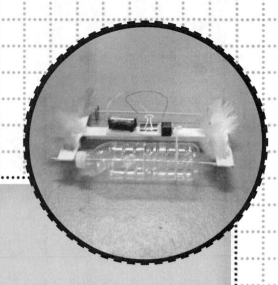

PARTS (Basic Car)

- Glue gun
- Drill
- End Mount Roach, 1 C battery
- Binder clip
- 2 paint paddles
- Drinking straw
- Water bottle with cap
- Rubber band, long enough to fit loosely around the bottle.
- 2 bamboo skewers
- 2 wheels (film canister lids, checkers, poker chips, etc.)

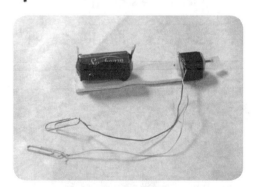

Start with the Roach, both wires with paper clips, and a hot glue nubbin on the end of the motor shaft. Two batteries will make it faster, but it really only needs one.

Drill holes about the same size as the skewer in the center of the lid and butt of the bottle. A large nail works well for a drill bit. It's OK if the holes are a bit bigger than the skewer, but it works best if it is snug in the holes.

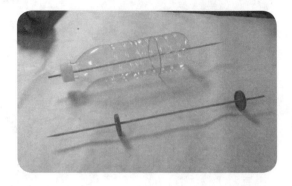

Thread a skewer through the holes. Drill similar holes in the two single wheels and thread the other skewer through them. Put the rubber band around the bottle.

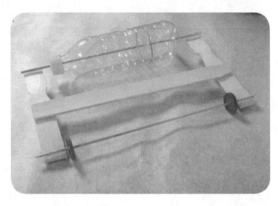

Cut one of the paint paddles in half and lay the pieces out in the arrangement shown. Set the two skewer axles into position and make sure they can reach both ends. When you've got all the lengths right, glue the paint paddles together. Snip off the end of the full-length paint paddle. This will be the chassis. Cut short segments of the drinking straw and glue them into position with the skewers' ends inside. The skewer should turn inside these straw segments. Ideally the straws should extend over the edge of the paddles so that if the wheels or the bottle shift to one side or another, they touch the straw first instead of the paint paddle. This reduces friction. Make sure everything spins smoothly.

The straws holding the axles should be on the bottom of the chassis. Clip the Roach into place on top. Snap the rubber band around the motor shaft, and adjust the Roach until the motor shaft is parallel with the axis of the bottle. Hook it up and see if it's turning.

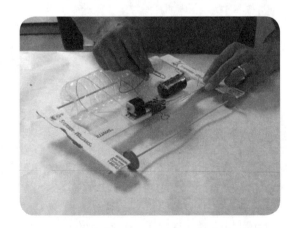

TROUBLESHOOTING

If nothing turns, your problem could be:

- Bottle is stuck—give it a spin to see that it turns freely

- Rubber band is too tight—stretch it or get a larger one

- Rubber band is dragging on the paint paddle—adjust the Roach so that it's not

If the motor turns but the bottle doesn't, your problem could be:

- Bottle is stuck

- Rubber band is too loose—adjust the Roach, reposition and glue the straw segments farther from the long paint paddle, or get a smaller rubber band

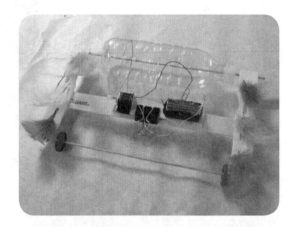

Decorate the Transmission Car if you want, and send it rolling across the room.

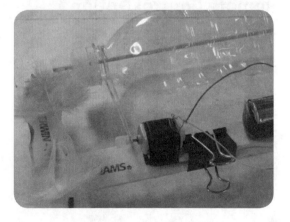

This car is called the Transmission Car because it has a second gear built in. If you turn the bottle or the Roach end to end, the rubber band can go around the neck of the bottle. The circumference of the neck is around half the circumference of the bottle waist, so the rubber band needn't pull as far to get a full rotation of the bottle. The result is a faster car. Try it out! It is not as strong, you say? Check the Science section at the end for an explanation.

Don't stop! Many more options remain with this basic setup. How about an amphibious vehicle—one that goes on land or water? Remove the two skinny wheels and put another bottle in their place. Stick two or three duct tape tabs on the drive bottle, and voilà!

That's pretty nice, but to make it more streamlined, you can get rid of that other bottle, and put two small ones along each side. This paddle-wheeler works almost as well as the one in the Water Machine chapter of this book!

Remote Control Option

PARTS

- Drill
- Glue gun
- Transmission Car
- 2 Roaches, short, no batteries, end or side mount depending on the orientation of your car chassis
- 2 film cans or thread spools
- Double DPDT switch unit (pages 36–40), or a commercial one, with four long wires
- 2 medium rubber bands
- 2 binder clips
- Bamboo skewer
- Cork

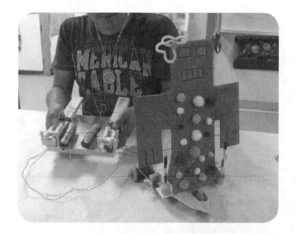

If you put two motors on two drive wheels, the Transmission Car can be converted into a very responsive remote control car, or proto-robot if you like. The robot shown here is built on a thin wood chassis that was cut out with a scroll saw, but you can build onto the same paint paddle chassis without much trouble.

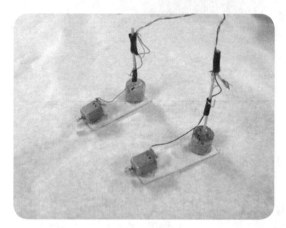

Make two short Roaches without batteries. Add small upright half skewers, mounted on half-corks, to keep the wires away from the turning wheels.

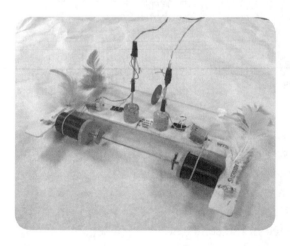

Drill holes, larger than the bamboo skewer axle, into the lids and bottoms of two film cans. Put these wheels on in place of the other two wheels. They will spin on the bamboo skewer axle, so you can glue it straight to the chassis now without straw segments. These will be the drive wheels, so put a rubber band around each. Put one of the old rear wheels on the front bamboo skewer in place of the bottle. Clip the Roaches onto the central paint paddle and line them up so that they will drive the rubber bands around each of the film canister wheels.

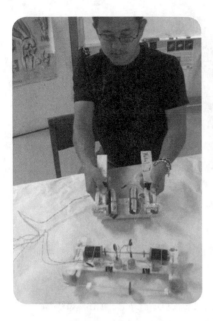 

Hook up the double DPDT switch unit and cruise the neighborhood.

The car should go forward when both motors are going forward, reverse when they are both in reverse, turn gently when only one motor is going, and turn sharply when one motor is going forward and one is in reverse.

If you have a coping saw, or a scroll or jig saw, you can make the chassis any shape that you want as long as you leave a place for the wheels and places to clip the Roaches. Here you can see a bicycle spoke glued across the back in place of a bamboo skewer. The film cans spin easily on the spoke and stay in place with cardboard tabs (glued only on the outside!). The front wheel is a film canister lid with a toothpick through it. It is mounted in the center hole with a segment of straw on either side glued under the chassis. It spins easily too.

Clip the Roaches into position. You can see that this car uses Side Mount Roaches. This gives a bit more adjustability for getting the tension of the rubber band correct.

Now hook up the switches and see if everything is working. When it is running smoothly, add your body and decorations: robot, monster truck, Lamborghini, or whatever you want to remotely pilot around your house. We used a cup to hold up the robot body.

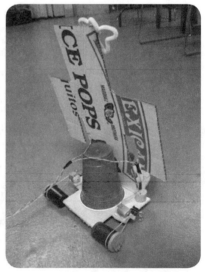

The Science Behind It

The transmission here and in the Two-Wheeler will be used in other projects in this book as well. As laid out in the section on Mounting the Motor, transmissions can change the speed and force of rotation from the motor shaft. On this car it is critical that the force at the wheels be stronger than a direct drive arrangement, such as on the Three-Wheeler. Having the driven shaft (bottle or film can) much larger than the driver shaft (motor shaft) makes this happen.

You may ask, "How do I make it strong *and* fast?" The answer is, "Forget it, buddy." If you want that, start shelling out some money for a better motor and a fancy battery, or go straight to internal combustion motors. Adjusting the transmission will always have its cost: more speed = less torque, more torque = less speed. This is one of the many laws in physics that come under the heading, "Life Is Hard."

You may also think to ask, "What if I made the driven shaft small and the motor shaft larger?" You could do this easily by putting a cork directly on the motor shaft, or even a segment of glue stick, and then putting the rubber band around this larger shaft. You can try this, but it is not likely to work for the following reason: increasing the size of the driver shaft will make the motor even weaker. In theory, it will also result in a faster driven shaft, but in reality, that only happens if there is any force to turn it. If not, you get nothing, and a soon-dead battery. The motor turns rapidly already, so if you want a shaft to turn even more rapidly, you'd best get another motor made for that specialty.

Staff and students at the Mission Science Workshop and the Fresno Community Science Workshop worked up a version of this project with an aluminum can in the mid-90s. They're still waiting to be paid for all the advertising they've been doing for the soda companies.

Water
Machines

Have you ever thought about why so many large cities are near bodies of water? Water is useful, and not just for drinking. You can haul stuff easier through the water because friction is low at slow speeds. It is always relatively level, so you don't have to deal with going up and down hills. If it is hard going up a river, you make up for it coming back down. And you don't need wheels, though you can make use of them in the form of paddlewheels and propellers.

Think of all the ways to make something go in the water: rowing, paddling, kicking, and spinning a propeller. You can "push" off water or the air above it. An enormous range of hull designs are possible. Your little hobby motor just happens to work even when submerged. The biggest problem you've got is that hot glue often comes undone when wet, but you'll soon learn how to get around that one.

Airboat

PARTS

- End Mount Roach, with 2 AA batteries and a medium to large propeller
- 2 cups or another mechanism to elevate the Roach
- Boat hull (wood or Styrofoam)
- ½ paint paddle
- Medium binder clip

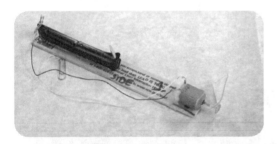

Start with an End Mounted Roach (page 22) and a propeller 3 or 4 inches in diameter. Make sure it's blowing well, though the direction it blows doesn't matter much.

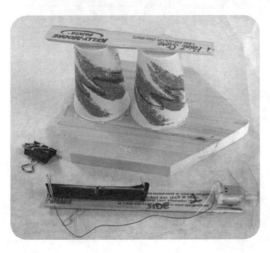

Make a boat base out of a chunk of wood. Drop it in water to make sure it floats—a lot of wood these days is made of sawdust or thin layers of wood glued together. It not only doesn't float well, but it also comes apart if it sits too long in water. You can also use Styrofoam for your hull. Put the other paint paddle up on something, such as two cups, so that the propeller can turn without hitting the water or the hull of the boat.

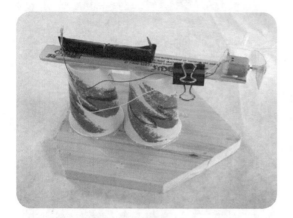

Clip on the Roach and propeller and you're ready for action. You can make the propeller pull or push the boat through the water. Check out which orientation gives you a more stable, straight ride. You don't need much water for this—I've seen it go through shallow puddles. Try this also on snow or ice, or even on a set of low-friction wheels.

You can slap a Roach on almost anything that floats to make an airboat. My students have done that on many occasions. Heck, you don't even need the Roach, and you can add as many motors as you want. If you have a toy airplane, borrow the propeller and see if it works any better than our homemade ones.

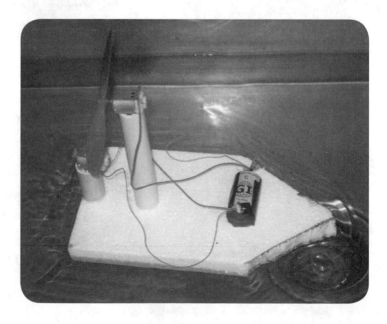

The Science Behind It

Airboats are really useful in swamps. Generally, it's more efficient to push off water than air if you want to move a boat (see the next project). But when the water is shallow and full of weeds, scum, and gators, it's better to have a smooth base on your boat so as not to tangle the propeller or rudder.

Real airboats use propellers as large as airplane propellers, all wrapped in a protective cage to keep them from sucking in and chopping up debris, birds, small people, and other stuff. Some use airplane engines and can go quite fast. It is a trick to steer or stop these things—remember, there is nothing but a flat bottom skimming along the surface of water. Steerage usually happens with vertical vanes directly behind the propeller. On this model, you can actually turn the Roach to change the direction of force.

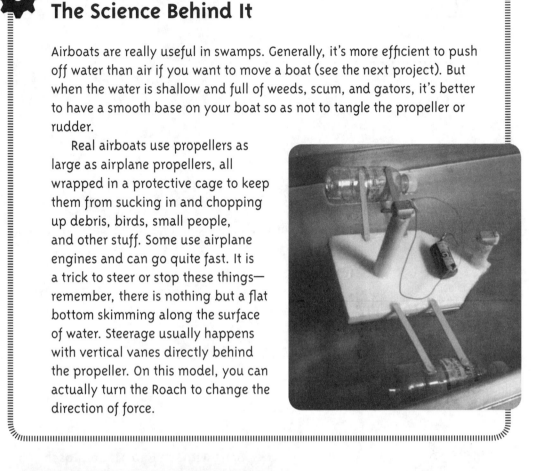

Manuel Hernandez, director of the Fresno Community Science Workshop, first turned my attention to airboats as a solution to dealing with the enormous one-inch deep puddles covering his park in the rainy season.

Motorboat

PARTS

- Knife or scissors
- Glue gun
- Drill
- Tape
- End Mount Roach, 2 AA batteries, with small propeller on a 4-inch section of hot glue
- Boat hull made of Styrofoam or wood
- Cork or film canister
- Rubber band

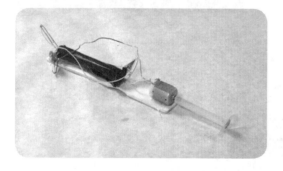

Start with the End Mount Roach (page 22) with a tiny propeller at the end of a glue stick shaft.

Cut a boat hull out of a piece of Styrofoam or anything else that floats. Glue the cork or film canister to the top.

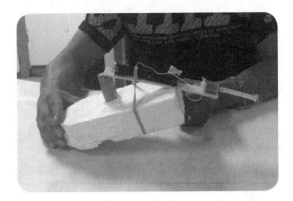

Fasten the Roach with propeller onto the boat with a rubber band. You could glue it, but remember two things. First, water will soak into the wood and unstick the glue. Second, you will want to tinker with the position and angle of the propeller to maximize power and control direction.

Turn it on, chuck it into the bathtub, and watch it make a wake!

POINTERS:

- The propeller should be under the water, but ideally the motor will not be. If it gets wet, it may fall off the Roach. Black tape it or rubber band it back on.

- If the boat moves backward, you can either redefine the back of the boat to be the front or reverse the wires on the battery. You could bend the propeller the other way, too.

- If the propeller flails wildly, take the glue stick segment off the motor shaft, snip off the part you drilled the hole into, and try to drill it again straighter. This is a real trick, so it may take you a few times to get it right. You can test it by turning the motor on before you put it in the water, but it is even harder to get a segment this long to spin smoothly in the air. In water, it spins slower and tends to be more stable. You could also try using a piece of wooden dowel instead of a glue stick.

- You should be able to control the direction by moving the back of the Roach from side to side under the rubber band.

Once it's cruising in the tub, find a bigger body of water! When finely tuned, this just may be the fastest machine in the book. You can make it turn slightly and watch it do loops in a pool or pond. You could even rig up tiny water skiers, if you're clever.

As you can see here, the Air Boat can be rigged as a Motorboat, too.

If you're hungry for more speed, you can mount dual Roaches. If you're clever, you can engineer them so that they turn in opposite directions, thus canceling out any sideways forces that may result from the rotation of a single propeller.

The Science Behind It

Isaac Newton's Third Law describes how boats (and everything else) go: for every action (water being thrown back) there is an equal and opposite reaction (the boat going forward). When you push on something in order to get going, you don't want that thing to move. Think about running in the sand—it's a pain, because every time your foot pushes off, the sand gives way a little and you waste a bit of energy. But when a car pushes back on a street surface, the street doesn't move much, as a rule. Water does move a bit, but not as much as air. This is why most boats, including the largest ocean-going vessels, have propellers under the water, pushing back on the water.

You only need a tiny propeller to make this kinetic contraption cruise. Check out some propellers, or pictures of them, on airplanes and boats. A motorboat with a propeller less than one foot in radius can be strong enough to pull a couple of water skiers. On the other hand, the propeller on a tiny airplane, even an ultralight, will be a good 2 feet long. The shapes are different as well.

This is all due to the different properties of gases (such as air) and liquids (such as water). Air moves easily when you push on it, and it is 1,000 times less dense. That is to say, a given volume of it is 1,000 times lighter than the same volume of water. The bottom line is that you have to throw a lot more air back than water to get the same forward force on a vessel.

Paddlewheeler

PARTS

- Knife
- Tape
- Glue gun
- Side Mount Roach, with 1 or 2 C or AA batteries
- 2 paint paddles
- Bottles, single-sized, 2 with caps
- Rubber bands
- 2½-inch pieces of PVC, 1½ inches long
- ¼-inch dowel, 12 inches long
- Thread spool or film canister
- Medium binder clip
- 2 plastic knives

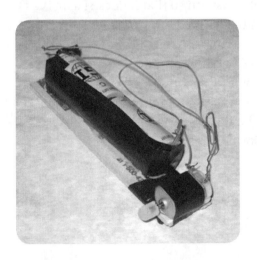

Start with the Side Mount Roach (page 22). It is best to keep it short. You may want to tape the motor on in addition to gluing it, since it will come loose if the glue gets wet.

Build the frame by assembling four half-paint paddles as shown. Chop two 1½-inch lengths of PVC and glue to the tips of the parallel paddles.

Strap on two single-sized drink bottles using rubber bands. They can point either direction—your choice—because the paddlewheels can paddle in either direction. The bottles will slip through the water better if the skinny neck end goes first.

Thread the dowel through the PVC segments with a spool or film canister in the center. Tape or glue the spool into position so that it doesn't spin on the dowel. Don't forget to loop the drive rubber band on there. Wrap rubber bands around and around the center of the knives, then thread the tips of the dowels through the rubber bands. If you're clever, get the wraps of rubber bands criss-crossed on the knives, which keeps them from slanting in one direction or another.

Now mount the Roach. Slide it back and forth, side to side, until it is perfectly in line, with the proper tension in the drive rubber band.

Pick the Paddlewheeler up, connect the motor, and see if the paddles spin. If not, continue adjusting. If so, break a bottle of ginger ale on it to christen it the good ship Knife-Paddler and drop it in the drink. Only then will you know if the balance is right. If the batteries are too far forward, you may need to reposition the bottles to keep the support under the weight. You may need to reposition the paddles if they are hitting the bottles, too. In fact, you can count on a good bit of repositioning before you're ready to conquer the high seas with this little boat. But once it is finally tuned up, it clips right along.

You can also make the body and hull from wood or Styrofoam or something else that floats. Just leave space for the paddles and the transmission system. The photo here shows a design that used a thin piece of wood on top of a thin piece of

Styrofoam. Since it's lower than the original design, the paddles plunge deeper into the water each time. It's unclear if this is a good thing—though they push on more water, it requires more force to lift them out on each rotation.

The Science Behind It

You may have seen photos of the grand paddlewheelers plying the Mississippi. The first steam-powered boats in the late 1700s all used paddlewheels, even to cruise across the Atlantic Ocean. Propellers were tried and sometimes used together with paddlewheels, but they did not effectively replace the paddlewheel until a hundred years later. It is useful to compare the two systems of propulsion. Both give forward force to a boat by pushing water backward, but that's where the similarity ends.

A spinning propeller is more efficient than a paddlewheel because it never comes splashing out of the water. It is also much smaller and simpler, allowing for less loss from friction when moving through the water. However, the complex curvature required of an efficient propeller is difficult to design and fabricate. Paddlewheels, on the other hand, are essentially a series of sturdy, flat plates that are easily made. As you can see from comparing this project to the Motorboat, a complex mechanism is required to transfer the power from the motor to the paddlewheel. A propeller, in contrast, can be stuck right on to the end of the motor shaft.

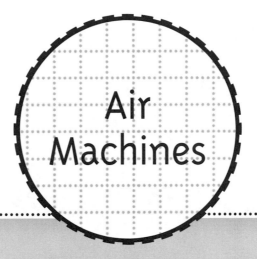

Air Machines

With a typical, cheap hobby motor and a normal battery, it is almost impossible to make an aircraft that flies itself through the air. Sometimes you can get some helicopter-like action if you put a large propeller on a naked motor and run thin wires to a bunch of batteries in your hand. But this kinetic contraption is hard to control and not particularly interesting. The following projects, on the other hand, are quite interesting. They may be a bit tricky to get running, but hey, *you're trying to make something fly!*

Basically, you can get an aircraft of any shape to fly around in circles at the end of a stick, and you can get a flat figure of your choice to fly in a giant circle hanging from the center of your room. You can make something float on a cushion of air, which is a different physical principle than a helicopter employs. Easiest of all, you can make a variety of small, light objects fly in a vertical wind tunnel, called a Windtube. This is exactly what aeronautical engineers do before they make a real aircraft.

Windtube

PARTS

- Glue gun
- Knife or scissors
- Transparent tape
- Motor with propeller of plastic or cardstock
- Battery pack, 2 or 3 C or D batteries
- 2 connection wires
- 4 or 5 two-liter bottles
- 2-x-4 baseboard about 8 inches long
- 3 tongue depressors or craft sticks
- Nails
- Stiff paper or plastic for the propeller
- Stuff to throw in:

  Salsa cups

  Styrofoam packing peanuts

  Plastic from bags

  Ribbons or tape from cassettes

  Thin string

  Paper balls

  Cardstock helicopters

  Tiny parachutists

  Whatever the heck else you can think of

Start by building a tube. A large piece of stiff, clear plastic is easy to roll into a tube and tape securely. This is hard to find, though, and expensive to buy when you do find it. Instead, you can use four or five two-liter bottles. First, cut off the bottom and top of each, leaving the central, tubular part. Cut a slit up one side of each. Then find a cylindrical salt box or another can or tube slightly smaller than the two-liter bottle and tape one of the slit tubes back into a tube wrapped around the cylinder. Be sure to use transparent tape.

Put the next one on, overlapped by about an inch, and tape them together.

Add the remaining bottles, moving the tube up as you put each new bottle on.

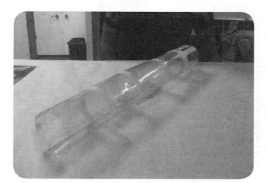

Glue tongue depressors or craft sticks upright to three sides of the baseboard, as shown. Put in two nails near the center so that when the motor is attached to them, it is centered inside the tube.

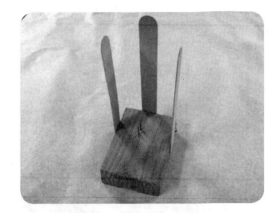

Rubber band or tape the motor to the nails. Make sure the motor is raised a bit and that the base end of the motor shaft is not touching the baseboard, or it will introduce friction and make the motor run slower. Put a fan onto the motor shaft. The one shown here is made from an old restaurant menu, but you can use bottle plastic or stiff paper.

Hook up the motor to a couple of batteries. Rubber band or tape the tube into position.

Connect the motor, get the direction right, and make sure there is a blast of air coming out of the top of the tube.

Once running, you are ready to start tossing things into the tube. Shown here are some things you can put into your Windtube. Bits of paper, plastic from bags, and corn-based packing peanuts are nice because they are easily modified with a twist or squeeze of your fingers.

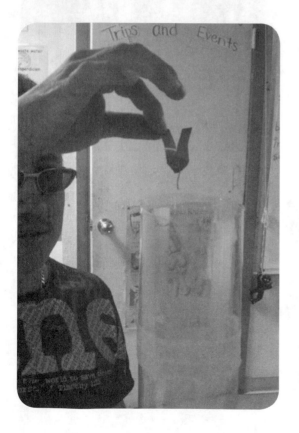

You can drop them through the top of the tube, or shove them in from the bottom just above the fan.

Three things may happen. The object
may go flying out the top of the tube,
fall down and smash into the propeller,
or float in the middle of the tube. Your
mission, should you choose to accept it,
is to modify the shape, size, or weight of
the object so that it floats in the middle.
This salsa cup floats in the middle, but
only after cutting off its rim.

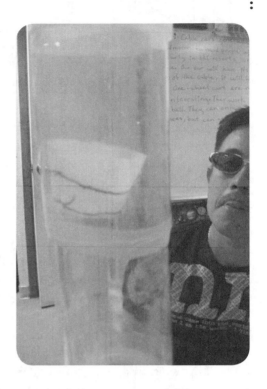

You can also craft a miniature parachutist and adjust the weight until she floats.

If you can't get even a small bit of paper to float, adjust your propeller and add
more batteries.

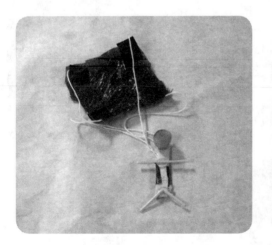

The Science Behind It

Obviously, the motor itself is not flying in this project, but it is making other things fly. To float in one place, an object's weight must not be greater than the force upward due to the wind. At the same time, if the weight is not enough the object will go flying out the top of the tube. This is a simplified version of the give-and-take problem that all aeronautical engineers must surmount when building a flying machine. In stable horizontal flight, upward force (lift) and downward force (weight) must balance perfectly. If one is greater, the aircraft will soon be accelerating either up or down. This is Isaac Newton's Second Law, often expressed as the Sum of All Forces = Mass x Acceleration, or $\Sigma F = m \times a$.

The PIE Institute at the Exploratorium has developed many great activities around large windtubes: www.exploratorium .edu/pie/library/windtubes/index.html. At the Watsonville Science Workshop, we realized that you can use a normal box fan and regular window screen instead of the hard-to-find flexible, transparent sheeting. Larger windtubes give more possibilities for exploration, but small ones are cute and more mobile. Take yours along to be the life of any party!

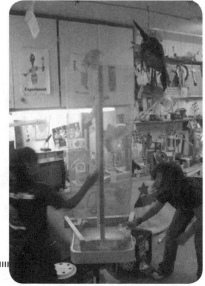

Gustavo Hernandez saw the large version of this at the Exploratorium and immediately miniaturized and perfected it for mass propagation. He's trying to cut back on soda, but not until he gets a few more bottles for this project.

Plane-on-a-Stick

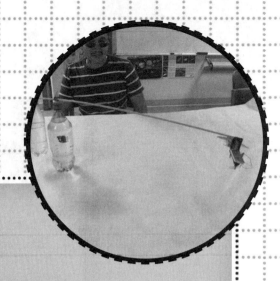

PARTS

- ⊙ Glue gun
- ⊙ Tape
- ⊙ End Mount Roach, 1 or 2 AA batteries, with propeller from bottle plastic
- ⊙ ½ paint paddle
- ⊙ Cork
- ⊙ Large bottle with cap
- ⊙ Smaller bottle with cap
- ⊙ ¼-inch dowel (or some other thin stick), at least 3 feet long
- ⊙ 2 small binder clips
- ⊙ Tack

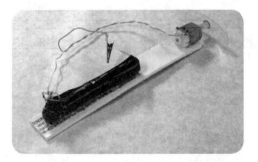

Start with the End Mount Roach (page 22). One battery may be enough, but two generates wicked speed. Stick a good-sized propeller on the shaft.

Make a plane, or any other thing that you'd like to see flying around in circles, out of half a paint paddle. Leave the bottom surface flat for clipping on the Roach. Glue a cork or half a cork in the center on top.

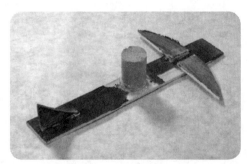

Glue one end of a ¼-inch dowel to the top of the cork, and the other end to the top of the smaller bottle's cap.

Reinforce the glue job on the cork with black tape if you think it looks shaky. Clip the Roach to the base of the plane.

Glue a tack to the bottom of the other small binder clip. Clip it onto the dowel near bottle cap.

Put as much water as you want in both bottles, the large one for stability and the small one for a counterweight. Move the binder clip back and forth until you can balance the stick first on your finger then on the tack standing on the cap of the large bottle.

Hook it up and let it rip.

Now you'll find out if the motor is going in the direction you planned. If not, reverse the wires, or proclaim you've invented the first airplane ever to have a reverse gear.

If you change the amount of water in the smaller bottle, you'll have to slide the binder clip with the tack in order to find the balance again. That will change the length of the dowel extending out in each direction. This can drastically change the speed—try it to find the speed you want. You can also try propellers of different lengths. This is a nice project to power with a solar panel if you have one. See the Getting Started section (page 5).

In 1998 I saw a large, elegant version of this project built by the kids at Rich Bolecek's Community Science Workshop, the Brookdale Discovery Center in Oakland.

The Science Behind It

There are two speeds physicists talk about when something is spinning; for example, a stick on top of a bottle. One is called the angular speed, or rotational speed. This is sometimes expressed in revolutions (times around) per second. It can also be expressed as the inverse, or seconds per revolution. This is called the period. It is not hard to measure this. If it's going slowly, you can just watch a clock or stopwatch and find out how many seconds it takes to go around once. If it's going fast, your limited reaction time may screw up the measurement. In that case, measure the time it takes it to go around 10 times. Then divide by 10 and you'll find out how many seconds (or what fraction of a second) it takes to go around once.

The other speed, called linear speed, you are most familiar with. The speed of a car or a baseball is given in units of distance/time, such as miles/hour. That's a linear speed. Even though this plane is traveling in a circle, it has a linear speed. You can calculate this linear speed, too. First, find the radius (in inches) from the support tack to the center of the plane. Multiply this by two to get the diameter, then by π to get the distance (the circumference) of the circular path it travels ($C=\pi d$). Then do the math with the results from the first experiment:

distance/time = speed
circumference/seconds to go around once = speed

The answer to this will be in units of inches/second, a linear speed. You can compare it to the speed of a car. My Plane-on-a-Stick went around 10 times in 9 seconds and had a radius of 22 inches, so I calculated that it was going about 150 inches/second or about 8 miles/hour. Twenty-five miles/hour (neighborhood driving) is around 400 inches/second, so this is slower than a very slow car. In other words, it won't lift off anytime soon.

Now, if you're still game, you could change the amount of water in the counter balance bottle, move the support tack, and do the calculations for this different flight path. Ahh, sweet, sweet physics!

Hovercraft

PARTS

- Glue gun
- Scissors
- 2 corks
- Hobby motor
- 2 AA batteries
- 2 brass fasteners
- Medium binder clip
- 2 connection wires
- 2 small paper clips
- Propeller made with playing card on a glue stick segment less than 1 inch long.
- Styrofoam plate
- Pencil or ballpoint pen

First make a battery pack (pages 16–17) of two AA batteries tightly taped together.

Now make a propeller. In this project the propeller is made from a playing card, cut the short way. It is thinner than a piece of bottle plastic, and is easier to make perfectly symmetric and to make small adjustments to. Glue then tack on the card strip exactly in the center. If you see that it is not in the center, or if it vibrates a lot when you turn the motor on, you can always trim off the longer side with scissors.

Mark the plate where you'll glue the two corks on at either end of the battery pack, as shown below. You'll want this exactly centered on the plate for even weight distribution.

Glue a motor to the binder clip exactly as shown. One handle should be glued to the body of the clip so that the clip will still open when squeezed.

Clip that binder clip to the center of the battery pack, then carefully push the propeller assembly onto the motor shaft. Bend up the edges to make it blow air, as described in Mounting the Motor (pages 25–27).

Another precision step: hold the batteries over the points where you'll glue the corks and make a mark below the shaft of the motor.

Now draw a circle around that center point with a diameter just larger than the playing card propeller. This is where the air will blow into the Hovercraft. It will be offset from the centerline that goes between the two corks. (It is less important that the air enter at the center of the Hovercraft and more important that the weight is centered.)

An easy way to cut out this circle is to draw around and around it with a pencil or ballpoint pen until it pops out.

Now turn the plate over and glue two corks onto the plate just above the two marks you made earlier. The corks may need to be cut down a bit—they should be about 1¼ inches tall. Unclip the motor and glue the battery pack to bridge the tops of the corks.

Clip the motor and propeller back on and adjust it so that it will blow straight down into the hole with minimum air loss. Hook it up and be sure the propeller is not hitting anything. You may need to adjust:

- The size of the hole

- The size of the propeller

- The height of the corks (although the binder clip allows for some adjustment in height)

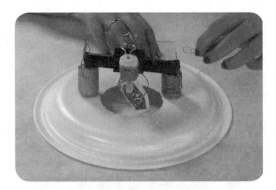

Check to be sure it is blowing downward. If not, switch around the wires. If it is blowing down weakly, bend the tips of the propeller down a little more.

Set the Hovercraft down and see if it will hover! It will only rise a bit, but with a gentle push should glide smoothly along until it hits something. It will work better on a perfectly smooth, flat surface. It may start spinning, too.

TROUBLESHOOTING

- If you hear the card propeller whacking into something, adjust the motor with the clip until it is centered between the corks and over the hole. If you can't get it to stop hitting, trim the sides a bit more, but make sure they end up symmetrical.

- Pick it up and point the bottom at your face. If the air is blowing down but just a little, bend the propeller blades up a bit more, but make sure they are symmetrically bent.

- Make sure your plate is not warped or bent. Some Styrofoam plates are better than others.

- Make sure the weight is not off center. If the Hovercraft always drags on one side, you can put weights, such as pennies, on the opposite side.

- The batteries must be fresh and well connected to make this one work. If you've been flying it for a while, expect it to stop working as the batteries run down.

You can also try to fly it on water, where most hovercraft are flown. I have achieved short flights on water, but the moment the plate touches the surface, the water adheres to the plate and you're sunk, both metaphorically and literally.

The Science Behind It

Hovercraft have propellers blowing air downward, just like helicopters. But you'll never see a hovercraft flying high above a city. These two machines work on fundamentally different principles. Helicopters work on pure Newton's Third Law: for every action there is an equal and opposite reaction. Essentially, a helicopter is strong enough to blow enough air down to provide enough force to support its weight.

A hovercraft is not nearly that strong. Instead of just blowing down, the propeller on a hovercraft forces air under the "skirt," in this case the rim of the plate. When a bit of extra air goes under the plate, it raises the pressure there, and begins to escape. The escape route is all around the rim of the plate. So the air escaping from under the plate provides a cushion all around for the hovercraft to float on.

Because of this, hovercraft can only travel on a smooth surface. Water is one place you can find a fairly smooth surface. Roads are smooth too, but before you begin work on a road-worthy hovercraft consider two things: stopping and turning. If you're not touching the road, it's really hard to do these things accurately, and if you can't, you're going to have a problem getting license plates for your machine.

Gustavo Hernandez and I went back and forth banging our heads on this design for more than one year. We finally succeeded, and for less than $2.

Flying
Caterpillar

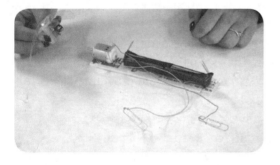

PARTS

- Glue gun
- Knife or scissors
- End Mount Roach, 2 AA batteries
- Propeller on glue stick mount
- Thick paper
- Kite string, thin cotton
- Paper clips
- Fishing spinner joint (optional)
- Ribbon (optional)

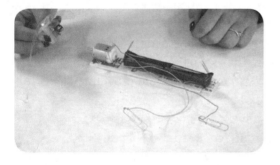

Start with an End Mount Roach (page 22) and a fairly large propeller. It works better if the Roach is as short as possible.

Make a caterpillar (or whatever other long, narrow creature you wish to fly) from thick paper. Glue it on the Roach such that the motor and propeller stick out well in front of the paper.

Cut a piece of kite string around four feet long and tie a paper clip onto one end of it. Find the point where the caterpillar will hang more or less balanced, but pointing upward slightly. Poke the paper clip through the paper at that point, and hang it up to make sure it is right. If not, try it again. We screwed up several times on this one before we got it right. Find a place in the middle of a room to hang it, but don't damage your ceiling doing this!

Connect it up and be sure the propeller is blowing air back across the body of the caterpillar. (If it's not, reverse the wires or tweak the shape of the propeller.) Launch it around the circle that you expect it travel in. It was a real trick to photograph this Flying Caterpillar. Once it's working well, you can put a ribbon on its tail, which looks cool flying around.

TROUBLESHOOTING

⊙ Be sure there is plenty of air blowing back over the Roach.

⊙ Most times these critters have a preference to which direction they'll go. It can be impossible to make it fly in one direction, but easy in the opposite direction. However, it is difficult to predict which way will be the easy way until you try both.

- Try launching the Flying Caterpillar at different angles, different heights, different speeds, and with different lengths of string.

- Make sure the Roach is pointing slightly upward. We found this to be key, and this seems to make sense; once the critter is flying around on its side, an "upward" angle will aid the circular motion, while a "downward" angle will be working against it.

- Make sure the string is not wound up tight. If it is, try using thinner string or use the fishing spinner joint.

The Science Behind It

Isaac Newton is at work here again. The Flying Caterpillar goes forward because it's blowing air back. If it's going backward, you can bet it's blowing air forward.

This project traces out a cone in your room, the tip of which is the tether point on your ceiling. The cone may be broad or narrow, but most times there is a certain shape that is most stable. The axis of this cone is an invisible line from the tether point straight down to the floor of your room. The motor shaft is spinning perpendicular to that axis as it travels around. In other words, there are two parts to the rotational motion here: the spinning motor shaft with propeller, and the caterpillar going around and around.

When things rotate, they generate interesting forces called *gyroscopic forces*. You can feel and see these forces in action with a toy gyroscope, a spinning bicycle wheel, or a top. When the caterpillar is flying in one direction, the gyroscopic forces are working with the propelling force of the propeller to make it fly stably around its path. In the other direction, these two forces are working against each other.

I continue to be fascinated with this project. I've seen hundreds of these built, and most work, but sometimes I can fiddle with one for a long time and still can't quite figure out why it doesn't work well. The gyroscopic influence is large, and, like various other factors, it is mostly invisible.

I first saw a cheesy plastic version of this on sale in an airport for something like $23. I rose to the challenge: this one costs me approximately 96 cents.

Spinning Machines

Up to this point, the projects in this book have only been concerned with going somewhere. But you don't have to go anywhere to have a good time. A lot of cool projects are possible with the motor just spinning something—solid, liquid, or gas. You can use direct drive, or you can use a transmission.

The Roach itself can make various things spin, such as a propeller, a fan, or a color disk. Stick an impeller on the shaft and you can make all the water in a bottle spin. Make that same impeller a bit larger and it can stir the air inside a bottle hard enough to blow around drifts of Styrofoam snow. Finally, you can spin things on a stick, either with direct drive or through a transmission, and watch the loose parts fly outward according to the laws of rotational physics.

Fan, Color Spinner, and Top

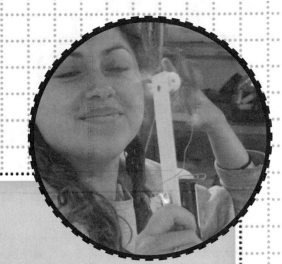

PARTS

- Scissors
- Glue gun
- Drill
- Side Mount Roach, 2 C batteries
- Clothespin switch, normally closed
- Large propeller on short glue stick segment
- White paper circles on stiff paper or thin cardboard
- Markers
- Hot glue or cork segments
- Film canister or other small plastic tube with a cap
- Tape
- Pushpin or long tack

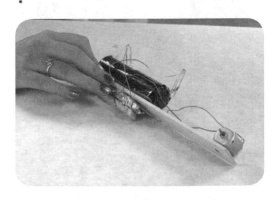

It doesn't get any simpler than this: three interesting things to spin with a Side Mount Roach. A clothespin switch, normally closed (page 33), is used here so your hand doesn't get tired as you fan yourself.

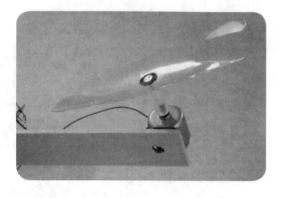

The first thing to spin is a large propeller. Check to see that it's blowing the right direction. If not, reverse the two wires. If it's not blowing much, bend the blades up a bit more, as described in Mounting the Motor (pages 25–27). You should be able to get a stiff breeze from this puppy. If it vibrates too much, that means one end of the propeller is longer than the other. Trim off the long end with scissors.

The second thing to set in motion with your Roach is a Color Spinner. Mount a circle of color on a segment of hot glue segment or cork. You can tack it, glue it, or do both.

You can make whatever pattern you want on the circle, and when you spin it the colors will mix together. To do basic color addition, put only two colors in radial patterns.

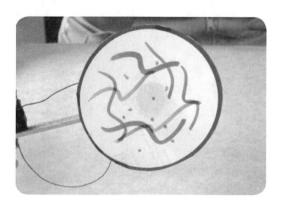

Finally, the trickiest one is the film canister top. Drill a hole, about ¼ inch in diameter, exactly in the center of the base of a film canister. Tape over it with three layers of black tape cut short so that they do not go over the side of the film canister. Poke a small nail hole through the tape.

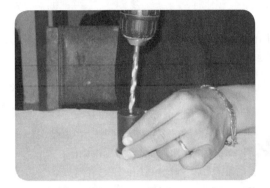
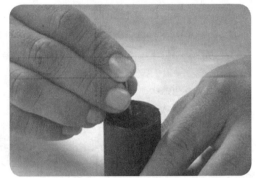

In the cap, poke the point of a pushpin or long tack through from the inside, again, exactly in the center. Take it out, put some hot glue over the hole, and push the tack back in again so that it is glued in place. Alternatively, on some film canisters it works better to glue a tack to the outside of the cap, as long as you can get it precisely in the center.

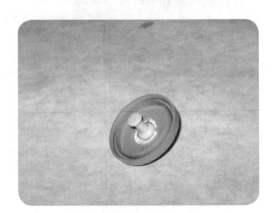

Now, put the cap on and gently hold the Roach in position so that the shaft of the motor is pressing slightly into the nail hole in the tape over the base of the film canister. Rev up the motor and watch the top gain speed. Smoothly pull the Roach upward, leaving the top to whirl away by itself on the table.

You can actually push the motor shaft down into the hole, hang the whole Roach a bit above the table, get it spinning, and then wiggle or bump it until it falls off.

The Science Behind It

Fans and propellers push air molecules. You can imagine the molecules are tiny balls standing in the circle of rotation of the propeller. The propeller blade swings into the balls, and they get pushed away according to the angle of the blade. If the angle is just right, they'll be propelled mostly straight forward. Other balls will move in to take their places and then be hit by the next blade to come around.

If the blade is at a severe angle, it will encounter a "thick circle" of air molecules and knock them all forward. The thicker the circle of air, the harder the motor will have to work to push them all. If the blade is at a slight angle, it will encounter a thin circle of balls, and the motor will not have to work so hard. The propeller will be able to go faster, but will not push as much air with each rotation.

Most propeller-powered planes can change this angle; they have what is known as a variable pitch propeller. This functions like an automatic transmission on a car to make the best use of the engine's force at any given speed. As a plane speeds up, the air moves past the propeller faster, so it needs to take a bigger bite of air to keep the same push, and thus the same engine speed. You can adjust the angle of the fan blades and feel the difference in how much air moves. Also, listen to the speed of the motor change as it has to work harder.

Color mixing in this project is quite interesting. You'll notice that when the circle stops, the colors are still separate. You may ask yourself then, "Where did the colors mix?" It was in your eye! This kind of mixing is fundamentally different than when you mix colors on paper. Try it: put two colors on a Color Spinner and mix them by spinning it, and then try mixing these two together straight on paper. You should get two entirely different results! If you want to read more about this fascinating phenomenon, look up color mixing by addition and subtraction, and the difference between mixing colors of light and colors of pigment (paint).

The Top is just a top like any other. If you get the top hole and the bottom pushpin exactly spot-on centered, it will spin steady for more than one minute.

My student Julian Mandujano invented the film canister top when he was in fourth grade. Chris DeLatour originally turned me on to the wonders of a spinning disk of colors.

Tornado

PARTS

- Drill
- Sandpaper
- Glue gun
- Hammer
- Nail
- Bottle (big is better) with cap
- Cup that the bottle can sit in, upside down, without the cap nearing the bottom
- Baseboard
- Motor
- Impeller on a glue stick segment, about 1.5 inches long (see Mounting the Motor, pages 25–27)
- 2 connection wires
- Aluminum foil
- 2 or 3 C or D batteries
- Color for the water
- Glitter, foam, and paper pieces
- Resistance wire (optional)

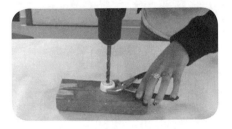

First drill a hole, around ⁵⁄₁₆ inch in diameter, in the bottle cap. Keep your pinkies away from the bit by holding the cap with pliers.

Rough up the top of the cap with sandpaper. This will help the hot glue stick to the plastic. Glue in the motor tightly, as shown. Put more glue around the edge to make a very strong connection. If you screw up on this part, the Tornado will leak. Furthermore, once it is wet, it just doesn't help to add more glue. You have to rip the whole thing apart, dry it out, and glue it again.

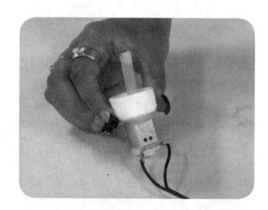

Hold on to the motor body (not the cap) and jam the impeller on the motor shaft. Strip both ends of two longish wires and hook one end of each to the motor.

Fold and wad some aluminum foil around one of the loose wire ends and tape it to the bottom of a battery. Make a battery pack (pages 16–17) with two or three batteries. Hammer a large nail into the corner of your baseboard and tape the stack of batteries to it. Glue the cup to the other end.

Fill the bottle most of the way up with water. If you want, put stuff in the water: food coloring, glitter, little chunks of Styrofoam, tiny bits of paper. Be careful not to add too much stuff or you could jam the impeller. You can always take the cap off any time you want and put in more stuff, or fish stuff out. Twist the bottle under the cap to attach it.

Press the loose end of the other wire to the top of the battery pack and watch it spin. Bits of Styrofoam will be sucked down into the whirlpool while glitter and paper bits will churn around and around. You can even get the vortex (whirlpool) to suck all the way down to the impeller where the impeller will create a small stream of bubbles.

The first picture in this project shows the wire connected directly to the top of the battery pack. But you can also make the current go through a length of the resistance wire and the motor will spin slower (see Peripherals, pages 40–41). It is a fun challenge to get a big chunk of Styrofoam to stay halfway down the vortex by moving the connection point on the resistance wire. You can also make little boats and act like you're taking them to the bottom of the sea.

TROUBLESHOOTING

If your whirlpool will not suck all the way to the bottom, there are a few things you can do:

- Add a battery
- Cut the impeller smaller, or a different shape; a smaller impeller will spin faster because it doesn't have to push as much water. As mentioned before, most small motors are built for high speeds, so most will be stronger when they're going faster.
- Take some water out
- Change bottles. Make sure to use a round one; small ones work, too, but you can't make as many interesting things happen inside as with a larger one

The Science Behind It

As the impeller spins the water around, it also flings it outward. When the water goes outward in the neck of the bottle it is also deflected back up. Thus there are two circles, or cycles, of motion happening simultaneously in the tornado. Water is going around in circles horizontally, like an ant walking around and around the hole of a donut. Water is also moving in a path down the inside of the whirlpool, out to the edge of the bottle and up, then back into the center and down. An ant walking down through the hole of a donut, over the bottom, up the outside, and down through the hole again, would be taking a similar route. These two motions are superimposed—that is, they are both happening at the same time. If you put a single bit of paper in the Tornado bottle, you can watch it trace out this path.

In this project, the bottle keeps the whirlpool turning around the center. A tornado or hurricane moves in a similar way, but it is a severe low-pressure area in the middle that keeps the air circulating around a central "eye."

The history of this project should be an ever-present lesson for all students and teachers. While single-mindedly pursuing a workable design for the Pump project, I sent a prototype to the Mission Science Workshop for trial. There, Paula Salemme found her students uninterested in building a silly pump, but several of them became sidetracked and put together a crude blender/toilet, which soon evolved into the Tornado. Over the last few years, we've built tens of thousands of Tornados across California, but only a couple hundred pumps. Moral? "Hey, teacher, leave those kids alone!"

Snow Globe

PARTS

- Scissors
- Glue gun
- Baseboard, 5 x 5, at least ½ inch thick
- Hobby motor
- Large impeller on a glue stick segment about 1 inch long (see Mounting the Motor, pages 25–27)
- 2 connection wires
- 2-liter bottle with cap
- CD
- 2 pipe cleaners
- Colored paper
- Stiff paper, as from a file folder
- Transparent tape
- Aluminum foil
- Styrofoam bits

Cut the bottom off of a two-liter bottle. Glue it to the baseboard.

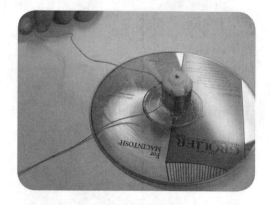

Glue a motor to the CD so that its shaft sticks up through the hole. Glue it securely, but take care not to get any glue on the shaft. Strip and connect the wires to the motor.

Holding the motor tightly, press the motor shaft into the hole in the free end of the impeller.

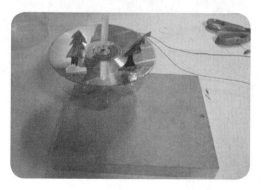

Glue the CD-motor-impeller assembly onto the two-liter-bottle base, as shown. Glue a few figures onto the CD, leaving enough space for the impeller to spin. Connect the battery to be sure the motor with impeller spins freely.

Cut the top part of the two-liter bottle down a bit (unless you want a tall Snowglobe). Do your best to make the rim straight and smooth, as it will need to seal down against the CD. You can tell if it is straight by setting it down on the table—it should stand upright with no cracks around the edge. Then cut two slits about half way up the sides.

Draw and cut out a figure from stiff paper and glue it onto a doubled pipe cleaner. Slide the figure up into the bottle top with the pipe cleaner sticking out of the slits in both sides of the bottle. Bend the pipe cleaner ends over. Use transparent tape to refasten the two slits together. Glue more figures against the back of the bottle if you want.

Set this assembly onto the CD and check if the impeller is still free to spin. Sometimes you have to cut the impeller shaft shorter or raise the pipe cleaner. You'd better get it right though, because the next step is to glue this whole assembly down to the CD. This is a trick sometimes, because the hot glue will often cause the bottle plastic to melt and deform a bit. It works well to put small dabs of glue all

around. (In welding, this is called "tacking.") If you still have big holes that the snow can leak out of, you can glue another pipe cleaner or a piece of thick yarn around the base to seal it. (This is not shown here.)

Set up a battery with a momentary contact switch right off the top and glue it onto the baseboard. Scrape little bits off a big chunk of Styrofoam and stick them into the bottle through the top.

Screw on the lid, connect the switch, and watch it snow. If you put too much snow in, you can dump some out through the mouth of the bottle. If you need to, you can try to adjust things by sticking a bamboo skewer down through the mouth, too.

Here's another model made from CD cases raised up on marker caps. The battery is hidden underneath. It was hard to get all the joints sealed, but it came out nice.

The Science Behind It

Propellers, which you find on fans, boats, airplanes, and helicopters, throw air forward or backward. An impeller, as found on this project, throws air outward from the shaft. Here the impeller powers a highly localized weather pattern; its blades push on the air. They also may strike a few pieces of Styrofoam snow, but the moving air pushes most of the snow.

The snow swirls around, showing us where the primary air currents are. You may notice snow getting stuck behind some of the objects you placed in the Snow Globe. These are areas of low wind speed. If you make a square or triangular Snow Globe, expect low wind speed in each corner, evidenced by a small pile of snow.

In a liquid snow globe, the bits of snow flow with the liquid instead of air. It may be smoother and more stylish, but your model is more realistic! If you want to make the wind blow in the opposite direction, switch the two battery wires.

At the Watsonville Environmental Science Workshop, we once taped together giant pieces of plastic to make a walk-in Snow Globe. We loaded it with hundreds of gallons of old Styrofoam packing peanuts. Then we put two vacuum cleaners in reverse to blow it full of air and then blow fake snow back and forth at each other. It's great fun, as long as you don't get Styrofoam stuck in your throat.

Thanks to Karla Hernandez, age 12, for the brilliant idea of a CD for this Snow Globe base.

Spinning Surprise Tree

PARTS

- Knife or scissors
- Drill
- Glue gun
- Baseboard
- Hobby motor
- Skinny cup
- 3 connection wires
- 2 tacks
- Paper clip
- Cork (needs to be solid and tight)
- Aluminum foil
- Decorations of your choice

Strip a couple of long wires at both ends and hook them to the motor. Drill a hole, about ⁵⁄₁₆ inch, in the base of a cup and glue the motor from the inside with the shaft sticking up through the hole. The shaft should stick up as far as possible and be free to turn.

Decorate the cup like Santa Claus (or anything else you want). He will be hidden by the branches of the tree and only visible when you start the thing spinning. If you use cotton, don't use too much because it tends to catch on the paper branches.

Don't glue the cup down yet. Rig up a two-C-battery pack and glue it down to the baseboard. Make a switch if you want. A two-tack paper clip switch is shown here.

Now for the branches: Poke or drill a nail hole in the cork. Push the motor shaft up into the cork hole, but be careful not to push so hard that the motor comes unglued from the cup. You can reach up and hold the motor while you push on the cork. It should go on as far as possible while still allowing it to turn without rubbing anywhere.

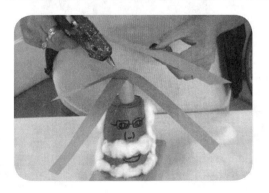

Cut the green paper into strips. Fold them in half and glue them onto the top of the cork, one by one, at different angles. Bend them down around the cup as you go, and continue putting them on until you can't see Santa.

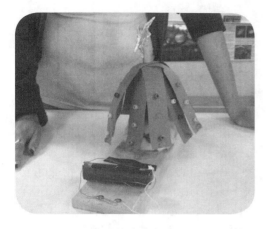

Decorate the tree. You can put whatever you want, but beads help to weigh down the branches and close it up when it stops spinning. Notice how there are a couple of beads at the tips of each branch.

All that is left is to trim the branches so that they don't hit the baseboard or the cup, and start spinning when you connect the circuit. Glue the cup down when everything is working right.

Here is a photo of a model using two stacked film canisters. One C battery happens to fit nicely in the bottom film canister, and the motor is mounted under the lid of the top one.

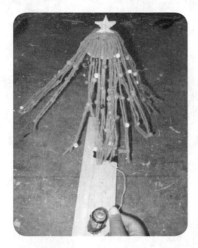

Here is yet another model, using green yarn instead of paper, without a cup and without Saint Nick.

The Science Behind It

You know what's going on here—you've already seen it at amusement parks and on merry-go-rounds. You also may recall being spun around in circles by someone when you were younger. The faster you spun, the higher you went. This is a rotational example of the first part of Isaac Newton's First Law: objects in motion tend to stay in motion. Furthermore, objects tend to go straight. When objects are going in a circle, look and you'll always find a force pushing or pulling them continuously toward the center of that circle.

The beads at the end of the branches are being pulled forward and around by the branches they're glued to. At every instant, they'll resist going around and attempt to go straight forward. The resulting force in the branches raises the beads and branches from a low position close to the center to a higher one farther from the center. This exposes the face of the dear old elf. Cute, and good physics to boot.

Spinning Pinecone

PARTS

- ⊙ Glue gun
- ⊙ Drill
- ⊙ Side Mount Roach, 2 C battery pack
- ⊙ Glue stick segment
- ⊙ 2 x 4 baseboard, about 8 inches long
- ⊙ 3 half paint paddles
- ⊙ 2 or 3 corks
- ⊙ Film canister or spool
- ⊙ 2 short segments of ½-inch PVC
- ⊙ Pencil, or ¼-inch dowel, sharpened at one end
- ⊙ 1 or 2 binder clips
- ⊙ Medium rubber band
- ⊙ Pinecone, or something to spin
- ⊙ Resistance wire, optional

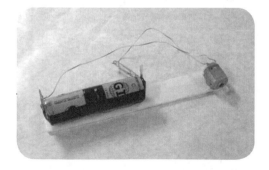

Start with the Roach. Leave some space between the batteries and the motor for the binder clip. Push a segment of glue stick onto the tip of the shaft.

Build an H-frame structure with the half-paddles on one side of the baseboard, as shown.

Put on two corks, and two sections of PVC, aligned vertically as shown. The lower one should be around a ½ inch above the baseboard, and the top one near the top of the pencil when you stand it up, leaving plenty of space for the pulleys in the next step.

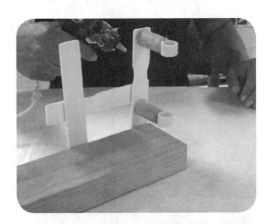

Drill a hole into the top and base of a film canister. The hole should be a bit smaller than the pencil so that the film canister grips the pencil tightly. If you use a spool, wait until after the next step and then glue it into position on the pencil.

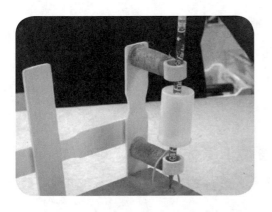

Sharpen the pencil or dowel. Thread the pencil through the upper PVC segment, then through the film canister, then the rubber band, and finally through the lower PVC segment. The pencil should be resting on its point.

Clip the Roach on the back of the crosspiece with the motor out over the end and the shaft sticking up. Hook the rubber band over the motor shaft and slide the film canister up or down until it's aligned with the shaft. Tweak the Roach until the shaft is parallel with the pencil. Hook it up and the pencil should whirl away. If it turns too fast, you can take off one battery, or you can use resistance wire to reduce it from full speed.

Stick something wacky on the top of the pencil. I had an old pinecone sitting around when some students and I came up with this project years ago, and it stuck. This is the rock-star version. If you use a dowel, you can make it as long as you want.

Make it go, watch it spin.

OPTIONAL

You can change the speed of this by adding more speeds to the transmission. You can drill a hole in half of a cork, and then thread the cork on the pencil just below the film canister.

Now, by sliding the film canister and cork up and down, the rubber band can go around the film canister (first gear), the cork (second gear), or directly around the pencil (third gear). Check out which gear is fastest and which gear is strongest.

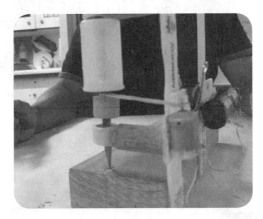

Here are several other beautiful versions of this project, courtesy of my students.

And for the grand finale, the Spinning Pinecone with Electric Lights! This design uses a couple of eye screws instead of the tubes for bearings, and a larger wooden wheel with a groove cut into it for the pulley. You can see the 9-volt battery strapped to the shaft and a circuit with a few holiday lights decorating the pinecone. Sweet, especially in the dark.

The Science Behind It

This is but a vertical example of the transmission used in the Transmission Car project (page 57). If you stuck the pinecone directly onto the motor shaft, it would not work as well because the motor is too fast and weak. The transmission slows the rotation down, and the motor is able to give more force, or torque. The larger the wheel on the stick, the slower it goes, and the more torque it gives. Connect straight to the shaft and you get some serious speed, but very little torque.

Bizarro Machines

This chapter contains a few projects that defy categorization. Not just land, air, water, or spinning machines, these projects have some of each.

A little hobby motor can power a small contraption that hops around crazily on the floor—not exactly transportation, but nearly as fun as a pet. A couple of motors can make circular waves in a suspended string, and also display properties of a wave you'll need to know for college physics. The same two motors in tandem will drive a small cab traveling quickly along a tight string from one place to another. You can use a motor with a small propeller to blow bubbles. And a tiny impeller will even pump water, allowing you to create stunning fountains, gurgling artificial brooks, or a cascade into your fish tank.

Hopper

PARTS

- Drill
- Glue stick
- End or Side Mount Roach, 1 A or C battery pack
- 1 or more paint paddles
- Cup
- 3 corks
- Baling or hanger wire
- Rubber bands
- Medium binder clip

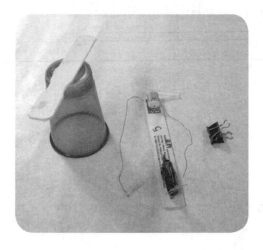

There are several ways to construct this popular project, some of which are described here. It's hard to see from the photos, but it hops around on the table like a hyperactive dog. Start with an End Mount Roach with only one battery (to make it lightweight). Drill a nail hole through the side of a 2-inch-long glue stick segment near one end. Push it onto the motor shaft. Glue a half paint paddle to the top of a fairly large cup.

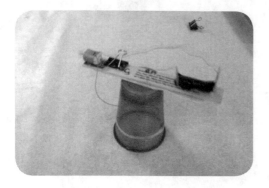

Clip it on, connect it up, and watch it hop like a maniac!

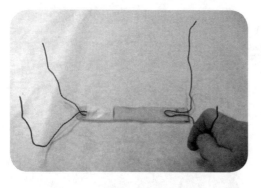

Here's another base made from two pieces of baling wire or hanger wire taped onto a half a paint paddle.

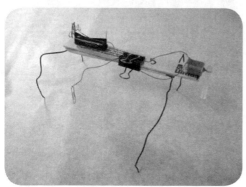

You can put as many legs as you want, and bend them in any shape.

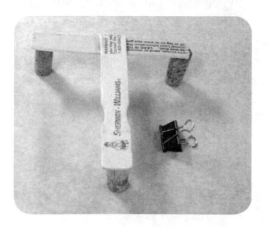

Another way is to create a base from two half paint paddles and three corks.

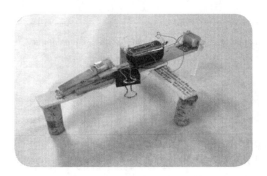

Shown here is a Side Mount Roach clipped onto the frame with a clothespin switch. Which end do you think should be the head? You can mount the Roach with the motor sticking off the other way, too.

This arrangement makes it easy to change the angle of the Roach and find out if you can control the direction it moves. I'm not going to tell you which way the Hopper moves in each of these photos.

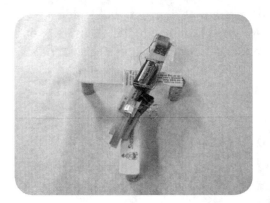

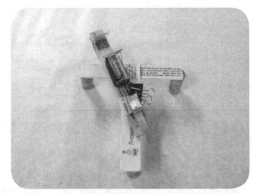

Finally, you can always tie markers to the legs of a Hopper and draw an interesting pattern on a big piece of paper. Use rubber bands to make it easy to switch markers in and out.

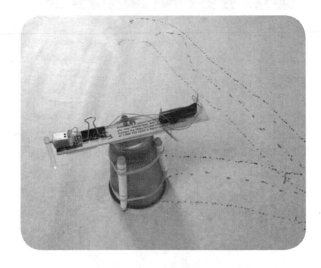

The Science Behind It

To understand how these hoppers hop, recall Isaac Newton's Third Law: for every action there is an equal and opposite reaction. When the glue stick swings left, the motor will move right. When the glue stick swings down, the motor will move up. And if the motor is attached to something, like the Hopper's body, it will drag that something along with it. The spinning glue stick is called an offset weight, and shows how most vibrators work, from foot massagers to cell phones.

You may have noticed that you don't see many vibrating vehicles like this moving down the road. If you found your Hopper difficult to control, you're not the first. It is unclear what determines its direction, but factors seem to be the shape of the feet, the direction of rotation of the glue stick, and the angle of the rotation in relation to the feet.

I first saw a hopper-prototype at the Mission Science Workshop in San Francisco in 1995.

Cable Car

PARTS

- ⊙ Glue gun
- ⊙ 2 Side Mount Roaches, no batteries
- ⊙ Battery pack, 2 AA batteries
- ⊙ Stub of wood, 1 x 2 works well, about 5 inches long with square ends
- ⊙ Cup, and passengers
- ⊙ String, long and strong

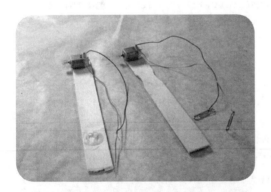

Start with the two stripped down Side Mount Roaches (page 22). Jab a glue stick nubbin onto the end of each shaft. Twist paper clips onto the ends of only one pair of wires.

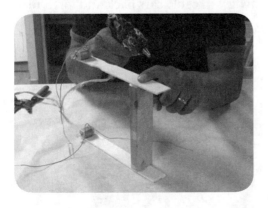

Glue the Roaches to the wood crosspiece, most of the way to the bottom, so that the motors are sticking off the same side.

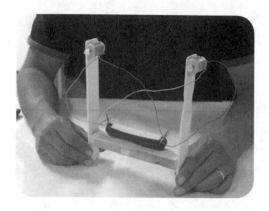

Glue a battery pack onto the top of the crosspiece. A PVC segment housing two AA batteries is shown here. Twist the two bare wire ends onto the two paper clips so that each paper clip is fastened to one wire from each motor.

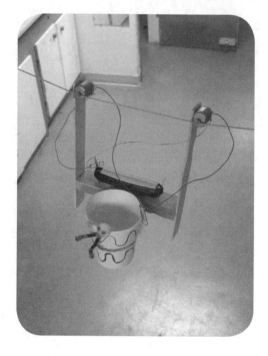

Glue on a cup gondola and make a passenger if you want. Hang it up, hook it up, and watch it take off.

If it doesn't take off like a racehorse, it could be that the two motors are spinning in opposite directions. In that case, reverse the wires on one motor. If you want it to go in the opposite direction, reverse the paper clips on the battery pack, or just take the whole thing off the string and put it on facing the other direction. This is one of the fastest contraptions in the book, and when my students and I discovered it we strung strong strings across the entire park and spent a happy afternoon sending passengers (candy, rocks, twigs) in cable cars back and forth to each other. You can also try to see how steep a hill it will climb.

Naturally, you can go nuts with the design on this one. Here is a photo of a Cable Plane by a pair of high school students from the Workshop.

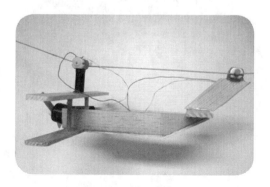

The Science Behind It

Vehicles that hang from a cable are also called aerial tramways or gondola lifts. They are rarely set up like this one for safety reasons: one bump of the cable and your car will plummet to the ground. Real ones are either locked onto a long loop of cable, or riding on one cable or set of cables while being pulled along by another cable.

Real life cable cars often take people and cargo across rough terrain. Once you go to the trouble to string a cable across a treacherous patch of land, it is ultra-efficient to travel along the cable. Like a train on a track, friction is low and the ride is smooth. You may ponder why you've never seen a cable car sitting on top of a cable. You're welcome to try to design one, and while you do, think how much easier it is to hang from a horizontal bar than to it is to balance standing on top of it.

Wave Machine

PARTS

- Glue gun
- Knife or scissors
- 2 Side Mount Roaches, ¾ of a paint paddle, long wires, no battery
- Battery pack, 1 C or D battery
- Shoe box, around 12 inches long
- 2 pushpins
- Thick string (woven is better than standard twisted)
- 2 medium binder clips
- 2 paper clips
- Resistance wire (optional)

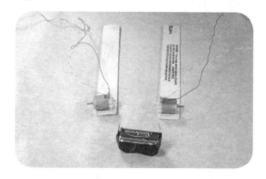

Start with two motor-only Side Mount Roaches (page 22), just as in the Cable Car (page 127) though a bit longer, and a single battery. Glue on the motors so they point in opposite directions.

Mount the bottom ends of the Roaches about an inch away from either end of the side of a sturdy shoe box. Punch a pushpin through from the outside of the box into the end of each paint paddle. The motors' shafts should be pointing toward each other.

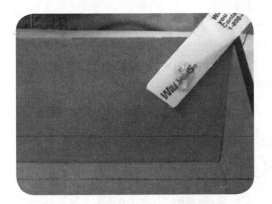

Squirt some hot glue over the sharp tips that protrude through the paint paddle. This will lock them into position and also make it safer. The arms should swing easily, side to side.

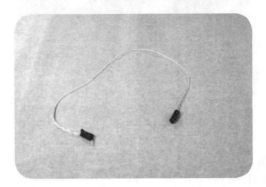

Cut a length of heavy string that just fits between the two motor shafts in their outermost positions. Make two stubby glue stick segments to connect to the motor shafts. Tape the ends of the string onto the two glue stick segments. The holes for the motor shaft should be on the tips.

Jam the glue stick segments onto the motor shafts. Twist the ends of one wire from each motor together and wrap them around a paper clip. Twist the other two wires in the same manner. Use the binder clips to clamp the Roaches to the side of the box. They should stay where you put them.

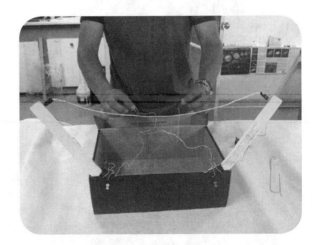

Glue the battery down inside the box and hook up the wires. You'll see immediately if you were lucky enough to hook the motors up so that they're turning the same direction. If you weren't, the motors will be opposing each other and the string will wind up tightly for a few seconds until everything stops. If this happens, reverse the wires to one motor. It doesn't matter which, because it doesn't matter which way the string swings. Once it's swinging smoothly, move the paint paddle arms to adjust the tension in the spinning string and try to get different wave combinations. Here are two full waves.

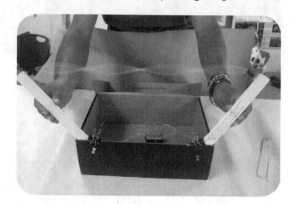

Here is a single wave.

You can also try restricting the spinning string by pinching it loosely in different places. Here is a wave and a half.

Sometimes you'll find odd patterns made up of the superposition of multiple waveforms.

You can put in a length of resistance wire to slow down the motor a bit to generate other waveforms. I've spent hours playing with this and learned a lot. It is cool to watch in the dark with a colored flashlight shining on it. If you happen to have a strobe light, you can see what the string looks like stopped. Of course, when you're done, you can fold down the arms and pack it all up in the box for mobile demonstrations.

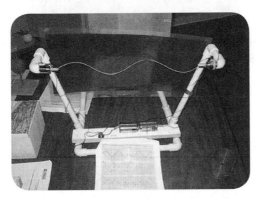

If you're keen on this project, you can make sturdier versions with PVC pipe or wood.

A related machine makes waves with one Roach and a string dangling down. These waves are a bit different, since the bottom can be held in one place or allowed to swing to the outside. Read the Science Behind It section on page 134, then check it out again: with this model, you can make ½ and ¼ wave multiples.

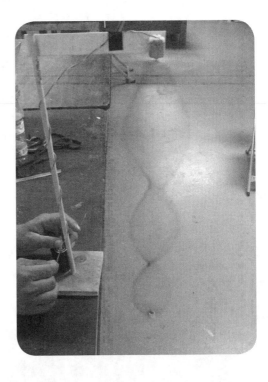

The Science Behind It

Waves are fundamental elements of nature. You'll need to study waves and vibrations if you want to understand earthquakes, music, complex electric circuits, atomic structure, light (and all other electromagnetic radiation), astronomy, explosions, and of course, the ocean. This machine makes an interesting, if quirky, sort of wave for you to get to know.

Waves formed by this machine are in multiples of ½ wave. A half a wave looks like this:

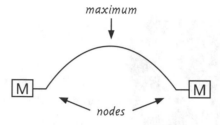

Spin it around and it looks like this:

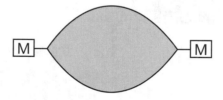

This is the waveform of a jump rope! This is also the "fundamental" wave of the Wave Machine, and it tends to be hard to achieve. Give it a shot. Since this is a half wave, the full wavelength of it would be twice the distance between the two motors.

A full wave looks like this:

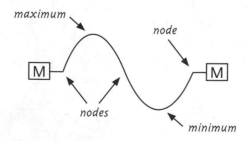

Spinning, it looks like this:

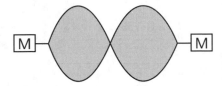

The wavelength of this wave is exactly the distance between the two motors.

Here are two waves:

Their wavelength is half the distance between the two motors. With this machine you should be able to achieve all these multiples of a wave:

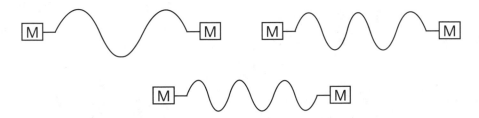

Waves move. Any drawing or picture of a wave is like a stop-action photo because it shows how things are at a given instant. But some waves, like the clear ones you can make on this machine, are called *standing waves* because their nodes, maximums, and minimums stay in place. It's a bit complicated to understand, but actually they're moving in both directions at once, bouncing off both ends and sitting right on top of each other. Chew on that for a while. This is what happens on a guitar string and inside a flute.

Thanks to Don Rathjen of the Exploratorium Teacher Institute for inspiration from his original fancy PVC model, which can be found in the incredible book *Square Wheels*, and also at www.exploratorium .edu/square_wheels/string_machine.pdf.

Bubble Maker

PARTS

- Knife or scissors
- Glue gun
- Tape
- End Mount Roach, C battery
- Momentary Switch, Normally Open
- Medium propeller on short glue stick segment
- Baling or hanger wire
- Yarn or pipe cleaners
- Bowl (for bubble solution)
- Bubble Solution:

    Dish soap

    Water

    Glycerin (if you can find it, but not necessary)

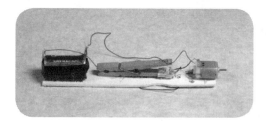

Start with the End Mount Roach (page 22). The momentary switch works well in the center.

Make a propeller and push it onto the motor shaft. Check to be sure it blows forward. If it doesn't, reverse the wires on the motor.

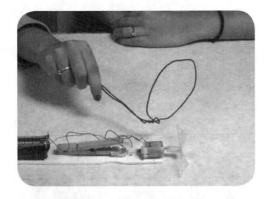

Form a loop about 3 inches in diameter from a piece of baling wire or an old hanger. Leave long tails on both ends of the wire.

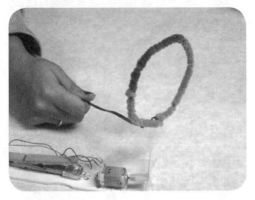

Wrap pipe cleaners or yarn around the loop. This will hold more bubble solution to the wire when you dip it.

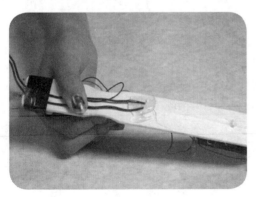

Tape and/or glue the tails of the loop onto the stick of the Roach. The loop should stick out a couple of inches in front of the paint paddle.

The loop should be parallel to the propeller's plane of rotation and about one inch in front of it. You want the air blowing through the loop. Keep bending the wire until it looks good. Put more tape on if it is still a bit loose.

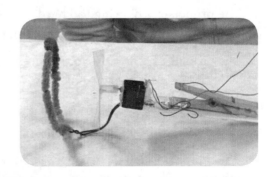

Pour some bubble solution into a bowl and dip in the loop of wire.

Pull it out and push the switch. You should get a bubble.

TROUBLESHOOTING

If it doesn't work, try it again. And again. Several more times. Still no luck? Here are some things to consider. If the bubble pops each time, there could be three things wrong:

- Your soap solution is no good. Try making bubbles with a straw or bubble wand. Make sure you can easily make good bubbles before you try making them with the Bubble Machine.

- The propeller is blowing too hard. Make it blow less by bending the corners down a bit, or snipping off the ends of the propeller to make it shorter.

- The propeller is too close to the loop. Bend the wire away from the propeller or slide the wire tails down a bit.

If the Bubble Machine spins but the bubble just stays tight across the loop, there could be three things wrong:

- The motor is going the wrong way. Make sure the air is not blowing back across the Roach. If it is, reverse the wires on the motor.

- The loop is too far from the propeller. Bend the wire so that it is closer.
- The blades of the propeller are not bent enough. Bend them so that they take a bigger cut of the air.

Some factors in making larger bubbles are a good bubble solution, patience, finesse, and moving the bubble ring so that the bubble itself doesn't have to move much. A small jerk up or down at the end does well to seal off the bubble. To make smaller bubbles you need a smaller loop and some mechanism to seal the bubbles off before they grow too large.

The Science Behind It

It is truly astonishing how much science is present in a common soap bubble. These bubbles are made of three substances: water, soap, and air. Water has a relatively large surface tension. This means the molecules of water stick tightly to each other. You can see this surface tension if you place a drop of water on the table. The drop will remain in a domed form, which means that its molecules enjoy their own company more than that of the molecules of the table.

Air is what the bubble is blown with, so to speak. With a drinking straw, you can blow bubbles in plain water, but they will usually rise directly to the surface and pop. The surface tension of the water is too strong to allow a bubble to remain at or above the surface of plain water. Soap lowers this surface tension and makes a freestanding bubble possible.

To get a bubble out of water you need to sustain a tiny layer of liquid. Scientists call this a *thin film*. When you put soap into water, it organizes the water molecules in such a way that thin films can form and bubbles can exist. The bubble wall is so thin it is close to the wavelength of light. Because of this, white light gets messed up when it goes through a bubble wall, leaving certain colors and canceling others. This phenomenon is called *thin film interference* and results in the wild rainbow of colors you see in a bubble. You can also see them in an oily puddle or an abalone shell.

This is yet another project I originally saw at the Mission Science Workshop in San Francisco.

Pump

PARTS

- Drill
- Knife
- Side cutter
- Glue gun
- Hobby motor
- 2 connection wires, 2 feet long
- 3 or 4 C or D batteries
- Aluminum foil
- Black film canister
- Flexible tubing, ⁵⁄₁₆ inch outside diameter, ³⁄₁₆ inch inside diameter, 18 inches long
- Tape
- Clothespin, spring type
- 2-liter bottle with cap
- Baseboard, at least ½ inch thick
- ¼-inch dowel, 15 inches long
- Small binder clip
- Rubber band
- Nail

Start by drilling a ⁵⁄₁₆-inch hole in the center of the film canister base. This will be the intake hole.

Drill a second hole in the side, all the way at the bottom. This will be the output hole.

Drill one last hole in the soda bottle cap. Get it precisely in the center. This plastic is much harder and thicker, so it is best to hold the cap with a pair of pliers and avoid getting your fingers too close. All three of these holes must be clean—pick away any burrs or loose plastic with a knife.

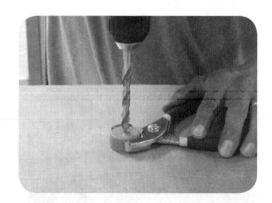

Pinch the length of tubing nearly at the end in the main indention of the clothespin.

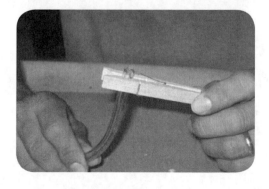

Insert the tip end of the tubing into the output hole on the side of the film canister. The clothespin should be tight against the side of the film canister with the tubing just barely protruding into the film canister. Tape the clothespin into position, leaving the tube untaped for further adjustment if necessary.

 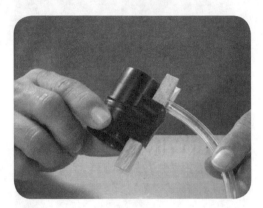

Stick the motor into the cap so that the shaft sticks out the top. It works well to put some glue around the hole, place the motor in position, and then glue all around the motor until the cap is half filled up with glue. If a bit of hot glue gets stuck to the shaft, pick it away when it's dry.

 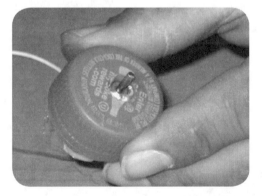

To make the impeller, cut a length of hot glue stick about as long as the diameter of the cap. Drill a nail hole through the center in the middle, then squeeze the tips with pliers until it looks like this:

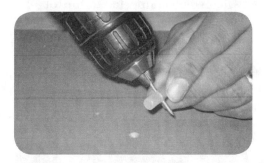 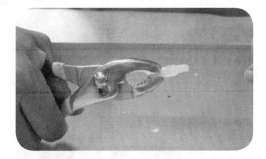

Push it firmly onto the motor shaft. Trim the ends with a side cutter until they don't stick out past the edge of the cap. This is the impeller assembly.

 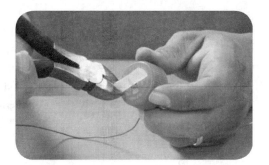

Leave those two parts for now and build the base. Any thick board will work. Drill a ¹⁵⁄₆₄-inch hole near the edge and hammer a ¼-inch dowel in. Decorate it if you want.

Stack up three or four batteries and tape them together. Wad some aluminum foil around one wire from the motor—it doesn't matter which one—and tape it onto the bottom of the bottom battery. Tape all the batteries to the dowel. The other wire from the motor will be the momentary switch when connected to the top of the battery.

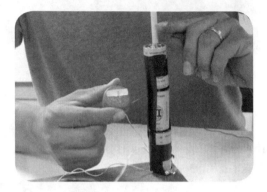 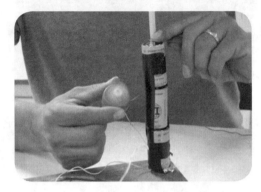

Now comes the tricky part: insert the motor assembly into the film canister. (This is much easier with the help of an assistant.) The Pump works, more or less, by the impeller throwing water down the end of the tube that is stuck into the side of the film canister. Thus, the impeller must be exactly even with the end of the tube leading from the inside of the film canister. If it's pushed too far it will be stuck against the base.

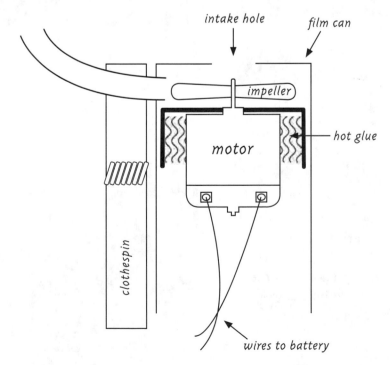

The best way to avoid this is by connecting up the motor so that it's spinning as you put it in. Then you'll hear the impeller make a different noise if it hits something. As you first slide it in, be sure it's not hitting the side of the film canister. If it is, trim a bit more off the tips of the impeller. Then, as it goes deeper, listen for it hitting the tube. If you hear that, ease the tube out from the clothespin a bit. Finally, watch closely through the hole in the base of the film canister and you'll see the spinning impeller approach. Stop when you see it exactly in line with the tube entrance.

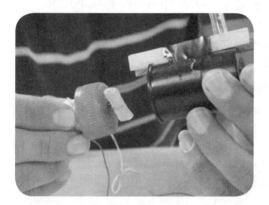
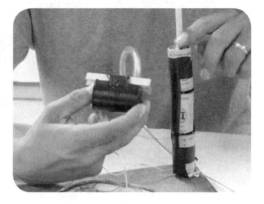

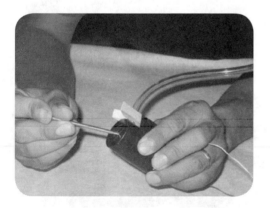

You will likely push the impeller assembly in too far, and the spinning impeller will hit the bottom of the film canister and stop. No worries. Get a large nail, poke it through the hole in the base, and push against the cap until the impeller assembly moves back down the film canister a bit.

Once the impeller is spinning crazily right at the entrance to the tube, the Pump is complete. Time to submerge it. Use any reservoir you have or cut the top off a two-liter bottle and fill it up with water. Drop the Pump in and jiggle it a bit to get the bubbles out. Air in the Pump will keep it from pumping at maximum efficiency. Then hook it up.

TROUBLESHOOTING

If water doesn't come blasting out like a fire hydrant, check for these possible pitfalls.

- Make sure the motor is spinning.

- Jiggle it again to make sure all air bubbles are out.

- Make sure the tip of the tube did not entirely fall out of the hole in the side of the film canister. If this is happening, you'll see water churning around the film canister, but not much heading down the tube. It should be no problem to stick the tip of the tube back into the hole in the film canister. Don't stick it too far in or the impeller will smack into it.

- Peer through the base hole and check to be sure the impeller is just in line with the tip of the tube. Adjust it up a bit with your thumb, or back a bit with a nail.

- You can enlarge the intake hole in the end of the film canister.

- If everything appears to be as good as possible, you may have to make a new impeller, as smooth and precisely as possible, then try it again.

Once you've got water spurting out, you can do any number of things to make a beautiful fountain. A small binder clip and a rubber band will hold the tube in position. Another binder clip is shown here holding the bottle in position next to the dowel. It is stuck in a slit cut into the rim of the bottle, clipped to the dowel.

You can also include a water wheel. Here is one made by gluing fins on a thread spool. The axle is a bamboo skewer spanning the rim of the bottle.

Or forget the whole bottle and use a bowl full of rocks for the reservoir. You can hide the motor under the rocks, just like the fancy commercial ones, and let the water gracefully arch over and hit the rocks. Strive for the serene gurgle of a gentle mountain stream, not the dull tinkle of a midnight potty run.

The possibilities with this project are endless: a forever-flowing river, a jet ski, a floating marble, or a fish tank fountain. I once saw an art installation in an elite San Francisco gallery that consisted of a pump just like this one pumping water to the top of a massive cascade. The cascade was made entirely from the plastic packaging shells you throw away after opening a new toy or tool or gadget.

The Science Behind It

This is called a submersible, centrifugal pump. This type of pump is widely used in industry. It made large-scale irrigation possible across the United States when farmers began to use it in the 1920s. Pumps like this also power most fountains and municipal waterworks.

I previously stated that the impeller throws the water into the tube. Here's a more concise explanation: when the impeller spins, it creates higher pressure at the wall of the film canister and lower pressure in its center. The intake hole in the base of the film canister is in the center, where there is low pressure, and the output hole is on the side where there is high pressure. Water is a fluid, and fluids tend to flow from high pressure to low pressure. Thus the water heads up the tube.

But the impeller throwing water is a perfectly good explanation. You may have seen an art toy made of a small table that spins. After sticking a paper plate to the spinning table, you dribble paint onto it and the paint makes beautiful patterns as it whizzes outward off the edge of the plate. If you've had the rare fortune to ride on one of the few merry-go-rounds left in this ever-more safety-conscious world, you'll know that you're always flung outward as it spins. Similarly, water flows off the tip of the Pump's impeller heading outward, that is, toward the wall of the film canister. Give it a hole to escape through and it will do just that.

Thanks to Amy Youngs for inspiration on this one.

Exploring Motors

With the stuff you've accumulated to do the motor projects, you can also do several simple activities that will illuminate many of the fundamental concepts of motors and the way electricity and magnetism are related. You can watch flowing current and a permanent magnet pushing on each other. You can wrap many winds of current around a core to create a larger magnetic field. And you can make the coil larger and watch it nudge a magnet when you put current through it.

You can also make a super-simple motor that spins fast. Then you can take apart one of your beloved hobby motors and look for the key parts inside. You can set up the type of motor first used to make continuous motion with interacting electricity and magnetism. And, as a grand finale, you can connect up three motors to show the function of a motor, generator, and meter all at the same time! Learn a bit of math and you'll be past the first-year electricity and magnetism course at your local community college.

Demos with Electricity and Magnetism

🔋

PARTS

⊙ Tape

⊙ Thin wire, 3 feet long

⊙ Magnet

⊙ Compass, or magnet hanging from thread

⊙ Battery

With just a few parts, you can recreate Øested's monumental discovery (see Introduction, page 2). Place the small compass on the table and observe which way it points. Tape a wire to the table running in the same direction. Put the compass on the wire so that the needle points right down the wire. Hook a battery to one end of the wire, and have the other end ready to connect to the other side of the battery.

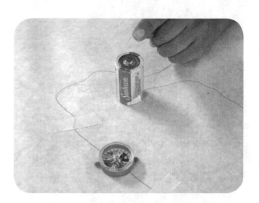

A compass is basically a magnet that is free to pivot; it will align itself with the largest magnetic field around. Before you hook up the wire, the largest magnetic field around is the Earth's. When you complete the circuit and the battery pushes a large current through the wire, that current generates a magnetic field that will push on the compass needle harder than the Earth's. The needle will deflect a bit to the side.

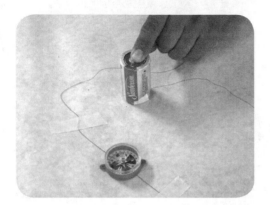 

This demonstration is proof of the connection between electricity and magnetism. If you don't have a compass, hang a magnet just over the top of the wire. Connect and disconnect the battery. (If you don't have a magnet, stop everything and go find one—a world of wonder awaits you!)

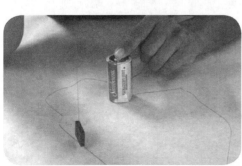 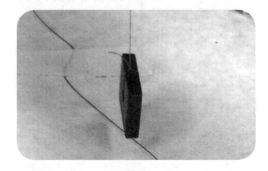

You can also do the converse demonstration. Place the wire so that a section of it is free to move. Place a magnet on the table just beside it.

Now connect the battery to make current flow through the wire. You should be able to see the wire jump. Turn the battery over and try it again. The wire should jump in the opposite direction.

This is a fairly weak push, but you can make it stronger by winding a wire many times. It's called an electromagnet.

Solenoid and Electromagnet

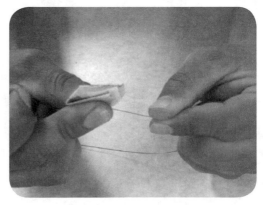

PARTS

- Scraper or sandpaper
- Tape
- Magnet wire, around 30 gauge, 6 feet or more
- C or D battery
- Paper clip
- Nail
- Straw
- Aluminum foil

Magnet wire is used in devices that need many coils close together. Its insulation is not thick plastic like connection wire, but rather a thin layer of paint or varnish. You need to scrape or sand this insulation off both ends before you can connect to it.

(You could do most of these activities with the same wire you use to hook up your motor, but they wouldn't work quite as well. The coils would be larger and more cumbersome, and the resulting electromagnetic fields wouldn't be as strong since each wind would be farther from its neighbors, making the magnetic field spread out more.)

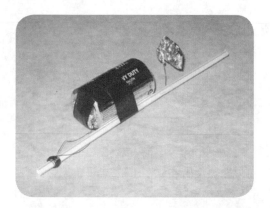

Wad little aluminum foil mitts onto each end of the wire. This makes it easier to connect to the tiny wire. Wind the wire around a straw right near the end. Hook up one end tightly to the battery, and use the other as the switch. Tape the battery onto the straw as well. This is called a solenoid, and can be used to suck in small objects with iron in them, such as nails or paper clips.

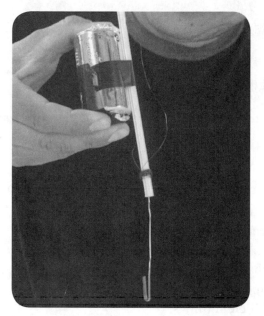

Unfold a paper clip or grab a nail, stuff it up into the hole, squeeze the battery to make a good connection, and see if you can hold it vertically without the object falling.

If you jam a large nail up the end of the solenoid, it becomes an electromagnet. Wrap some tape around the nail to make it stick in the drinking straw. You can pick up small objects with this, just as you can with a permanent magnet.

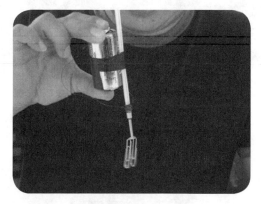

You didn't need the straw at all to make an electromagnet—you can just wrap wire directly around a nail. But it's nice to be able to pull the nail core out and have a solenoid.

So, a coil increases the magnetic field by packing wires with current close together. If you hang a magnet in the middle of a coil of wire, you get a meter.

Meter

PARTS

- Tape
- 1 D battery
- Magnet wire, 24 to 34 gauge, 6 to 12 feet long
- Cardboard
- Aluminum foil

Roll some magnet wire around a D battery to make a coil. Twist it together so it won't come apart. Strip the tips of the two ends as in the previous project, and leave them free to connect to different things.

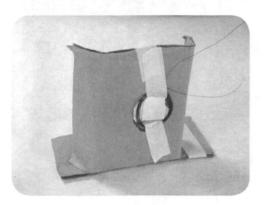

Make a simple cardboard frame with a hole in a vertical wall, as shown. Tape your coil into the hole.

Hang a magnet from a thread just in the middle of the hole.

When you hook up a battery to the wire ends, the coil becomes an electromagnet and the magnet hanging inside turns to align to this magnetic field.

This simple meter can be used to test batteries. Weak batteries will turn the magnet more slowly while strong ones will make it jerk to attention. It can also be used to show polarity. If you hook up the battery in the opposite way you get this:

With different polarity, the current is running in a different direction, so the electromagnet is formed in the opposite direction as well.

You may notice that this is not so satisfying. All it does is jerk halfway around and stop. There's not much work you can do with that, right? But if you're clever you can work out how to switch the wires each time the magnet comes around to give it another push and send it around again. Then you'd have a motor—like the next project.

Motor

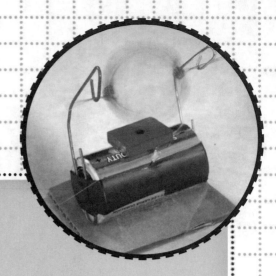

PARTS

- Knife or scissors
- Needle-nose pliers
- Tape
- Glue gun
- 1 D battery
- Magnet wire, 24 to 28 gauge, 6 feet long
- Magnet
- Cardboard or wood
- 2 large paper clips

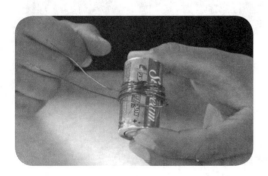

Here is a common, simple way to build a motor. The coil itself will turn, so it has to be perfectly symmetric and balanced. Wind some magnet wire, about 24 gauge, around the D battery.

Wrap the ends around the coil and leave them sticking out an inch or so. This will be the coil as well as the rotor. That means it will be the thing spinning. It must be perfect: symmetric and balanced with its ends as straight as possible.

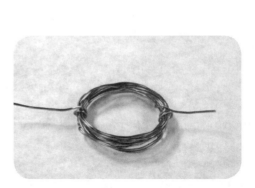

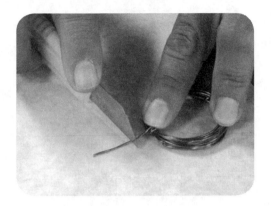

Now comes the sensitive part. Using a knife or scissors, scrape the insulation off one side of each wire end. This one-sided scraping serves the function of a "brush" in a normal motor.

The insulation should be missing from one side of each end. A close-up picture would look like this:

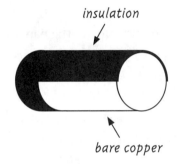

insulation

bare copper

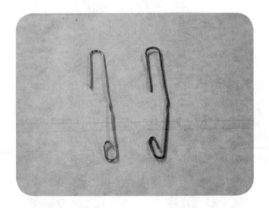

Get two paper clips and bend them as shown. Needle-nose pliers are useful in doing this.

Tape them tightly to the ends of the battery. Glue the battery to a piece of cardboard or wood, and glue a magnet to the top of the battery. (It may stick by itself—some batteries have iron in the casing, some don't.) Slide the coil into the slots.

If you are quite lucky, it will start twirling away. This happens in about 1 of 100 cases. All other cases must start troubleshooting.

- Give the coil a flick. Check to be sure it jerks a bit, which means that the magnet is pushing it. If it just turns like any piece of scrap metal, it means there is a bad connection somewhere. There are only four connections to check. The two at the battery can be made better by taping them more tightly, or clamping the battery between your thumb and forefinger.

  The two at the top of the paper clips depend on your scraping job. Scrape a bit more insulation off the ends of the coils if you are in doubt. In fact, you can scrape one off completely and leave half of only one insulated.

- The coil must be well balanced. Grab it like the photo here and twirl it a bit between your fingers. If you let go and one side always falls to the bottom, gently form the ends so that they come out exactly from the center of each side of the coil.

- Make sure the battery is not dead! If you leave the coil sitting in the paper clips when it stops turning, sometimes it is still connected and you'll drain your battery in just a few minutes.

- Sometimes the copper of the magnet wire oxidizes a bit overnight, which creates a chemical layer of insulation, so you may have to scrape the ends of the coil if you have left it for a while. Scrape the two crooks in the paper clip while you're at it to be sure they're not oxidized or covered with crud.

- Another trick is to take off the magnet and hold it in different positions on the side or top of the coil.

The way this motor works is hard to believe, but it's similar to all other motors. It is pushed and/or pulled around by the interaction of two magnets. One is the permanent magnet. The other is the coil itself, which becomes an electromagnet when current flows through it. If you've played with two magnets, you know that they naturally line up and attract to one another in a certain orientation. "Opposites attract, likes repel" is the rule at work here. The same is true for this pair of magnets: the coil (with current) will turn in its paper clip arms until its north pole is aligned with the permanent magnet's south pole, or vice versa.

On the other hand, if no current is flowing through the coil, it will follow Isaac Newton's First Law, that is, it will tend to stay at rest if it is already at rest, or stay in motion if it is already in motion.

So the stage is set. If everything is just right, it could work. When your motor is spinning merrily along, it means that the current is flowing at just the right time so that the coil electromagnet gives a nice shove off the permanent magnet. And then the insulation you didn't scrape off stops the current and the field and allows the coil to continue spinning around until it comes to the scraped spot again, the current starts, the magnetic field is created, and another push is given in the same direction.

Plenty of things can go wrong with this system, but if you keep on tweaking it, it will go. You can put a tiny piece of paper on one end of the coil arms to add bravado, but you'll have trouble making this motor do anything useful. Real ones are, after all, quite different.

By the way, if you haven't played with magnets much, put this book down, stop everything, put all your other plans for the day on hold, get some magnets, and play! Magnets are one of several areas of physics in which you can personally discover most of the basic laws without help from books or teachers. Just play, carefully observe, and then describe what you see.

Motor
Dissection

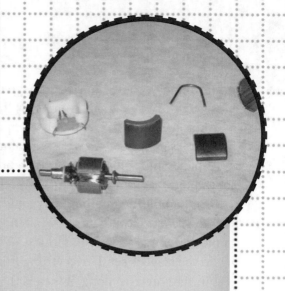

PARTS

- Motor
- Nail
- Needle-nose pliers

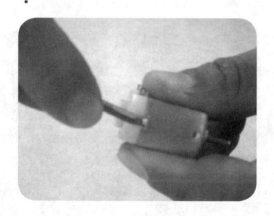

Carefully rip apart a commercial motor. With the one featured in this book, you can poke a nail under the small tabs holding the back tight onto the main casing and bend them up.

Pull it apart and look inside.

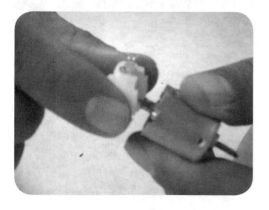

Pull out the shaft and look for the following parts

⊙ **Coils.** Many small motors, like the one pictured here, have three coils, each wrapped around a chunk of laminated metal core. This kind of metal supports a strong magnetic field and avoids eddy currents which can oppose the field.

⊙ **Central shaft.** The shaft usually sticks out of both ends of the casing through tiny bearings. The combination of the shaft, the coils, and the laminated metal chunks is called the rotor, and rotates. When referring to its electromagnetic duties, it is called the armature. Look for two wire ends to each coil and see how they attach to the tiny, segmented cylinder near the back end of the motor. The brushes rub there, making electrical connections and disconnections as the shaft turns.

⊙ **Brushes.** These feathery thin pieces of metal connect the wires coming into the motor to the rotor of the motor. They rub on the tiny cylinder described above, and only connect to two of these at a time, as shown in the diagram here.

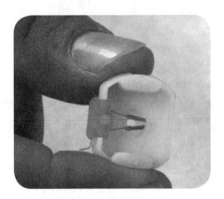

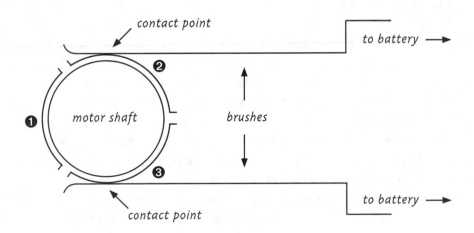

3 connections to coils = ❶, ❷, ❸

- **Permanent magnets.** There are usually two stuck to the sides of the casing. They will be arranged with opposing poles, often painted different colors for easy assembly. These and the casing are sometimes called the stator, and are stationary. Their purpose is to create a magnetic field for the armature to turn within. You can often rip them out by prying out a tiny spring holding them in position.

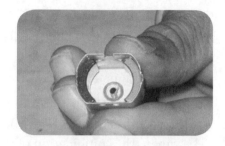

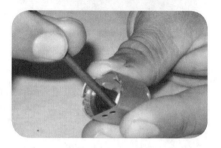

Whereas the stripped-down motor only gets one push per rotation, most efficient motors get many pushes. Three coils and two magnets mean an electromagnet is being pulled and pushed by the permanent magnets three times for each rotation. Stronger motors have an even more complicated arrangement that results in more and stronger pushes. You will also notice that the commercial motor has extremely tight fitting parts—the closer the armature is to the field-producing magnets, the less loss there is. The stripped-down motor described above is abysmal: one pathetic coil, one haphazard push per rotation, and all kinds of space between the magnet and the coil. There are many other models you can make that solve some of these problems and result in a better motor. Simon Field has some nice models in his book, *Gonzo Gizmos* (Chicago Review Press).

You may rip apart a motor someday and find no magnets at all. Unfortunately for us magnet-hounds, many motors in the world are not of the type we use in this book, that is, DC (direct current). Many motors don't need to move from one place to another, and thus can be plugged into the wall, which means a connection to reliable AC (alternating current). Most AC motors have no permanent magnets, but rather use coils for electromagnets on both the rotor and stator. It turns out to be more efficient this way.

These cheap little hobby motors are much more efficient and useful than the original motors made back in 1821. But you can learn a lot from building one of those.

Motor Current Use

When the electric car you just built hits the wall and stops, you'd best go disconnect the battery because the motor is sucking it dry. It just so happens that a motor not turning uses a lot more current than one that is turning. Before I explain how that works, take the Cable Car (page 127) as an example. There are two motors connected to one set of batteries in parallel. Connect them up and make sure they're both spinning. Now grab the shaft of one to stop it. Notice the other one slows down. This is not because it is sympathetic and wants its buddy to hurry up. It is because the one you stopped is hogging the current from the batteries and not leaving as much for the other one.

At any given instant, a motor's brushes are connected to the rotor and current is surging through its coils. With current, the coils become electromagnets and push and pull on the permanent magnets. If the rotor is free to turn, this causes it to rotate to a point where the brushes move to the next set of connections. The current stops, changes paths, and the resulting electromagnets then push and pull again on the permanent magnets. The rotor keeps turning and the cycle continues. This complex cycle, also involving something called "Back EMF," gives considerable resistance to the battery, limiting how fast electricity can be used.

If, on the other hand, the rotor is stopped, the brushes hold one set of connections and the current continues without stopping or changing directions. This is much easier, and gives less resistance to the battery.

Thus, the faster the motor shaft changes position, the more resistance the motor gives to the current flowing through it. A slower motor will have less resistance, and a motor that is stopped will have little resistance at all. Batteries go dead faster when connected to something with low resistance, since more current can flow. Moral: run, don't walk, to your car when it hits the wall. The life of its battery is in danger.

Homopolar Motor

The motors described in this book use two magnetic poles. The armature turns between the poles and the shaft rotates. The first motor to be made was actually of a different sort. It utilized only one pole of a magnet and had a current being pushed through that field. Such motors, called homopolar motors, are elegant but nearly useless. You can make one easily if you have some gold-plated neodymium magnets. If not, you'll need more patience and finesse, but it's still possible.

PARTS, FANCY MAGNET

- Gold-plated neodymium magnet ball or cylinder
- Nail or screw, 1.5 inches long
- Connection wire
- 1 AA, C, or D battery

If you have the fancy magnet, stick it to the head of a nail or screw. The point of the nail should then stick to the bottom of a battery and hang down. Run a wire from the top of the battery down to the magnet. Drag it along the waist of the magnet. The magnet and nail should begin to spin rapidly.

PARTS, NORMAL MAGNET

- 8 to 10 round magnets
- Connection wire
- 1 C or D battery
- Aluminum foil

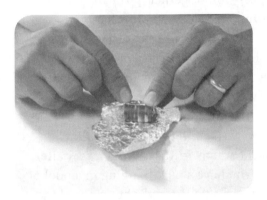

Wrap a short stack of round magnets in aluminum foil.

Stand a battery on top of the stack of magnets. Shape the wire such that it is supported by the tip end on the top button of the battery, and then coils gently down around the battery, as shown above. The other end of the wire should be brushing on the foiled stack of magnets. It should be free to spin, but always brushing a bit on the foil, thus connecting the circuit.

You should be able to get the wire to turn steadily, if not at a breakneck pace.

To understand how this type of motor works, think about the normal magnet version first. The magnetic field in this motor is oriented with one pole up. Thus the name "Homopolar," meaning single or one pole. Of course there is another pole—every magnet has two poles—but the wire does not need to approach it. The wire dangles past the top pole and into that magnetic field. When it touches the foil, a current surges through the wire, and is pushed by the magnetic field, always to the side, in the same direction. It pivots on the support at the top and continues to be pushed around and around.

The fancy magnet motor is a bit trickier. The current travels again through the wire, but now also through the magnet and the nail to get to the other pole of the battery. The magnet itself turns. This stumped me at first. I knew the current must be traveling through the magnet, but in all the motors I'd ever seen, the current and the magnetic field were in two different sections of the motor. After all, they have to push on one another. But here they are both together in the magnet.

Here's the key: while the magnet is turning, its field is not. It is hanging from one pole and is symmetric around that axis. As it turns, the field stays stationary. Therefore, the current in the magnet is pushing off a stationary magnetic field and giving torque to turn the magnet. I have yet to come up with a slick demonstration of this explanation (which a physics professor gave to me) but it does explain the movement.

At best, these homopolar motors are slow, weak, and unimpressive. But close your eyes and imagine you are Michael Faraday in 1821, about a year after electricity and magnetism had been linked. You have a wire hanging in a pool of mercury. You stand a large magnet so that it sticks up through the center of the pool. You know mercury is a conductor and you send a strong current flowing through the wire-and-mercury circuit. The wire begins to make lazy circles around the center magnet and doesn't stop until you stop the current. This is big stuff: finally, a way to get electricity and magnetism to make continuous motion— the beginnings of making it do work for us. The electric washing machine is still a few years, actually decades, off, but you know you're on to something.

Motor= Generator= Meter

PARTS

- Glue gun
- Nail
- Cardboard base
- Side Mount Roach, 2 C battery pack
- Side Mount Roach, no battery, alligator clips on the wires if possible
- Third motor with some sort of spinner to monitor shaft movement
- Cork
- Rubber band, fat
- Binder clip, large
- Lights, holiday and flashlight bulbs (optional)
- Meter, commercial or the one you made on page 156 (optional)
- Tape

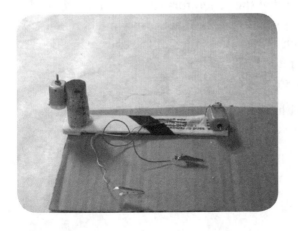

Glue the Side Mount Roach (page 22), with no battery, in the top corner of the cardboard as shown. Glue the cork to one end of it, and glue or tape the third motor to the side of the cork so that its shaft points straight up.

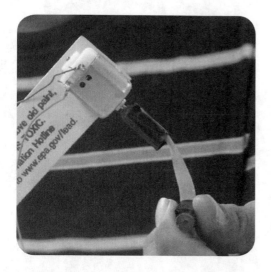

Clip the other Side Mount Roach to the edge of the cardboard so that the two motors are lined up, shaft to shaft. Connect them with a rubber band of just the right length taped at each end to a segment of hot glue. Put nail holes in the hot glue segments and jam them onto the two motor shafts. This is a flexible connection between the two motor shafts.

Stick something on the shaft of the motor affixed to the cork so that you can see how much it spins. Connect the two loose wires to this motor. When you turn on the Roach with the battery pack, its shaft should turn and cause the shaft of the motor on the other Roach to turn. Adjust the angle or tension of the rubber band to get it spinning as fast as possible. The motor on the cork should begin to spin. If it doesn't, try realigning the motors with linked shafts. You can always try adding more batteries, too.

If the spinner does spin, this is proof that the generator—the driven motor—is making electricity. The fact that the motor on the cork is spinning much, much slower than the motor on the first Roach means that much of the energy has been lost in the transfer from motor to generator and back to motor.

This project links everything in the section above.

◉ The motor on the Roach powered with batteries is simply acting as a motor: taking electricity and converting it to motion.

◉ The motor on the other Roach is acting as a generator: taking motion and converting it into electricity.

◉ The motor on the cork acts as a meter: it turns faster or slower depending on how much electricity it receives.

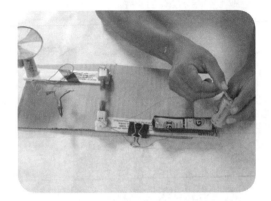

You can hook up other things to your generator. You wouldn't know it by looking at this photo, but I got a dim glow from a single holiday light when I hooked an additional C battery to the battery pack. I couldn't get any glow from a flashlight bulb, but that doesn't mean you shouldn't try.

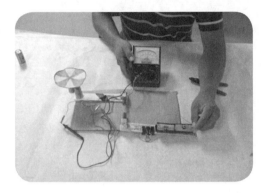

Connecting a commercial meter to the generator shows that it gives around 250 milliamps at less than one volt. That's pretty weak—no wonder the light didn't shine brightly.

Finally, I hooked up the crude meter I made earlier and it jerked responsively when the motor was connected.

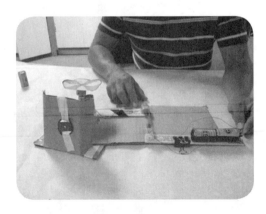

It's not much of a generator, I'll readily admit. But hey, it was built to be a motor, and we're getting electricity from it. I call that 100 percent magnificent.

Thanks to staff at the Exploratorium Teacher Institute for several ideas for making Homopolar Motors and the Meter.

Appendix: Supply Sources

Check my Web site, www.curtgabrielson.com, for information on ordering parts or kits.

RETAIL, SCRAP, AND DONATION SOURCES

Cabinet Shop or Lumber Yard: scrap wood pieces

Dollar Store: batteries

Electronics Store: motors, magnets, wire

Hardware Store: magnets, wire, tools, tape, fastners

Photo Shop: film canisters

Paint Shop: paint paddles

Phone Company Yard: wire

Radio Station: CDs and CD cases

Recycling Center: bottles, cans, old speakers for magnets

School Supply Store: paper, beads, glitter, food coloring, paint, googly eyes, craft sticks, pipe cleaners, pompoms

Second-hand Store: motorized toys for motors, wheels, toasters, etc.

About the Watsonville Environmental Science Workshop

The Watsonville Environmental Science Workshop is located within the Community Center at Marinovich Park, 120 Second Street, in Watsonville, California. It was founded in 1997 and is one of 12 such programs nationwide.

The Workshop is not only a broad after-school program, it is also unique community resource. The Workshop complements the science and math education students get from schools, and allows them to pursue their own interests. The Workshop gives local kids and their families the opportunity to explore together in a rich, stimulating, and safe environment with adults present who care about their development, not only in academics or science, but also as whole people.

The core of our program is the open-structure, open-door Workshop. After school and on Saturdays, community kids and their families are free to come and construct the projects of their imaginations. While they are here, they experience our exhibits and project models in addition to whatever project they choose to construct. They learn to use tools on a plethora of different materials, getting direct experience in science, math, and engineering. They get the opportunity to learn through inquiry, exploration, and peer consultation. The competence they gain builds true confidence. All the while, they are subconsciously defining "science" for themselves, and the definition involves fun and success. All this is markedly different from what most of them get in school.

In addition to the core Workshop program, we take our most popular hands-on science projects to around 18 local school sites through our Science

Teach program, in which lead teachers and high schoolers team up to do the teaching. The SH Cowell Foundation and other after-school grants through the Pajaro Valley Unified School District support the Science Teach Project. Two alternative high schools bring their classes to the Workshop once a week for a formal hands-on science lesson complete with notes and write-up. Several field trips and camping trips each year get students out into the local environment. We work closely with the other environmental education programs of the City of Watsonville. Teachers frequent the Workshop for informal consultations on how to succeed with hands-on lessons for their classes, and we occasionally do mass teacher training as well.

Our funding comes approximately two-thirds from the City of Watsonville and one-third from grants and school district support for our work with schools. Everything we do employs recycled, reclaimed, and scrap objects, so that students are made firmly aware of the value and potential of the materials around them. Conservation principles are conveyed, as well as the presence of science in everyday life: students become aware that science is everywhere, not just in special labs and kits. In addition, this practice keeps our costs low and our Workshop sustainable. We always welcome donations of interesting junk.

For more information, please contact us:

Curt Gabrielson
Watsonville Environmental Science Workshop
120 Second St.
Watsonville, CA 95076
Tel: (831) 768-3256
Fax: (831) 763-4018
www.ci.watsonville.ca.us/scienceworkshop

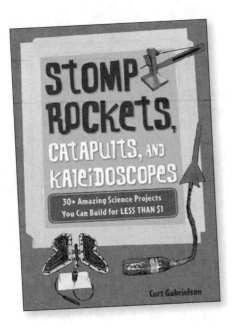

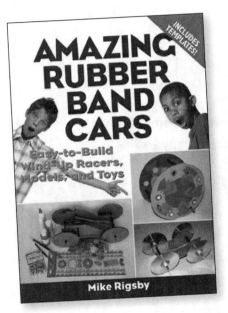

Amazing Rubber Band Cars

Easy-to-Build Wind-Up Racers,
Models, and Toys

by Mike Rigsby

978-1-55652-736-4
$12.95 (CAN $13.95)

"These projects are fun to construct, and inquisitive minds will be fascinated by the moving cars, whether done for a science project or strictly for leisure time enjoyment." —*School Library Journal*

There's no need for expensive construction kits if you have a handful of rubber bands, a bottle of glue, a pile of recycled cardboard, and a copy of *Amazing Rubber Band Cars*. Author and engineer Mike Rigsby gives kids what they need to know to build a variety of racers, including templates and step-by-step instructions. Once readers have built the basic rubber band car, they can modify their designs—replacing the wheels with discarded CDs, installing axle bearings made of aluminum foil, and improving the rubber band drives to make their cars go even farther.

Haywired

Pointless (Yet Awesome) Projects for the Electronically Inclined

by Mike Rigsby

978-1-55652-7791
$16.95 (CAN $18.95)

Unless you live in a haunted house, the eyes on your paintings probably don't follow you around. However, with a couple of motion sensors, two motors, a few transistors, resistors, diodes, and wires you can convert a Van Gogh print into a macabre masterpiece with a mind of its own. *Haywired* proves that science can inspire odd contraptions: Create a *Mona Lisa* that smiles even wider when you approach it. Learn how to build and record a talking alarm, or craft your own talking greeting card. Construct a no-battery electric car toy that uses a super capacitor, or a flashlight that can be charged in minutes, then shine for 24 hours. Written for budding electronics hobbyists, author Mike Rigsby offers helpful hints on soldering, wire wrapping, and multimeter use.

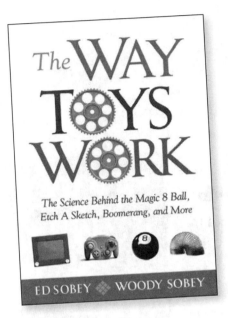

The Way Toys Work

The Science Behind the Magic 8 Ball, Etch A Sketch, Boomerang, and More

by Ed and Woody Sobey

978-1-55652-745-6
$14.95 (CAN $16.95)

"This book is sure to provide hours of entertainment and enlightenment."
—*School Library Journal*

How does an Etch A Sketch write on its gray screen; why does a boomerang return after it is thrown; and how does an R/C car respond to a radio-control device? Father/son author duo Ed and Woody Sobey explain the science hidden in these and dozens more of the world's most popular toys. Each of the 50 entries includes its history, patent application drawings, interesting trivia, and a discussion of the technology involved. The authors even include pointers on how to build your own using recycled materials and a little ingenuity and tips on reverse engineering old toys to get a better look at their interior mechanics. Readers will also enjoy photos of the "guts" of the devices, including a filleted Big Mouth Billy Bass. The only thing you won't learn is how the Magic 8 Ball is able to predict the future—some things are better left a mystery.

Gonzo Gizmos

Projects & Devices to Channel Your Inner Geek

by Simon Field

978-1-55652-520-9
$16.95 (CAN $18.95)

"Excellent." —*Science Books & Films*

Return of Gonzo Gizmos

More Projects & Devices to Channel Your Inner Geek

by Simon Field

978-1-55652-610-7
$16.95 (CAN $22.95)

Calling all tireless tinkerers! Author Simon Field has amassed a collection of science projects, from hydrogen fuel cells to vacuum pumps to computer-controlled radio transmitters. Learn how to take detailed plant cell photographs through a microscope using a disposable camera. In 15 minutes, build a rocket engine out of aluminum foil, paper clips, and kitchen matches. Or construct a geodesic dome out of gumdrops and barbeque skewers. Each experiment contains illustrated step-by-step instructions with photographs and diagrams to make construction easy. Organized by science topic, each chapter includes explanations of the physics, chemistry, biology, or mathematics behind the projects. Most of the devices are built using common household products, or components available at hardware or electronic stores. A few projects, such as a metal alloy that is liquid at room temperature, require a limited number of items readily available through science supply catalogs. No workbench warrior, science teacher, or grown-up geek should be without these idea-filled resources.

**Available at your favorite bookstore
or at www.chicagoreviewpress.com**